FIGHT FOR IT

FINANCIAL

The Fight for Financial Freedom Seen Through the Eyes of a Debt-Free Christian, Husband, Father, U. S. Marine and Police Officer

NATE JAMES

TESTIMONIALS

"Nate does a wonderful job outlining how his readers can pursue financial freedom in practical ways. He uses a great deal of Scripture as a guide and his illustrations from his time in the Marines and as a police officer are riveting and make the subjects at hand exciting, challenging, and motivating. I wish I had read this 30 years ago!"

Pastor Tom Zobrist, Senior Pastor at Liberty Bible Church, Author of *The Zobrist Family: Look What God Can Do.*

"I found Fight for it Financial to be different than any other finance book out there. I was entertained and the writer knew the challenges of law enforcement. I found it emotionally moving, humorous and alive with day to day reality in the life of a cop."

Danny Lynchard, Executive Director of the Tulsa Police Chaplaincy Corps, senior Pastor at The Father's House, and author of *The Heart Of A Cop.*

"We live in a world where common sense isn't common anymore. Thankfully, Nate James provides efficient wisdom for attaining financial freedom in a way that honors God. I wish I could give a copy of this book to 18-year-old me!"

Gunnar Hanson, Senior Pastor Grace Point Church, and retired U.S. Navy SEAL Team 3 member.

"I have finally read a book that reflects my views delivered with some common sense about finances, military service, duty, honor and relationships all rolled into one very well-presented volume of "Life 101" advice! I found myself being educated and informed, as well, as inspired. A Christian viewpoint that is not in your face dogma, but a book of love for family, country and God. A great book at so many different levels – a book that belongs on every family's home bookshelf. Worthy of a 5-Star Book Rating!"

Bill McDonald JR, Founder of *The Military Writers Society of America* & *The American Authors Association*. Vietnam War Veteran (*Distinguished Flying Cross, The Bronze Star, The Purple Heart*, 14 *Air Medals*.)

DEDICATION & INSPIRATION

The truths and life experiences in this book were written for my boys, who are very loved. I didn't sugarcoat them, because these experiences and stories portray the reality of life. Hopefully it will help them as they live their lives.

The inspiration to write this book came to me while thinking about a time when I was in college. My mom made a homemade cookbook containing all her favorite recipes. Being an immature college kid, I didn't think much of it, even though I really appreciated her for taking the time to make it for me. I thanked my mom, but sadly, I don't remember where the cookbook ended up. The meals I made at this point in my life were not gourmet, to say the least, and it was never used.

Unfortunately, my mom passed away about ten years later. I still miss her dearly. I tried to reconnect with her by finding old voicemails, but I was unsuccessful. I then thought about the cookbook. I searched high and low for months but never found it. There isn't much I wouldn't do to find that cookbook now. Her death was heartbreaking, but I learned a couple of vital lessons. First, life is fragile. Pay attention every day to what is important. Don't wait until tomorrow. Secondly, there will be a time when children aren't ready or willing to see the value in something extremely important. I don't know how old my boys will be when they're ready to absorb the information in this book, or if I will be around to help them when they are. Boys, when you are ready, know that I wrote this book for you first and foremost. I love you more than words can describe. My hope as a father is that this book will help you throughout your life. Please don't lose it!

This book contains financial insights and other lessons I learned from the Bible, from my parents, from my time in the United States Marine Corps, police work, time as a caddie, by spending time with other Christians, and by experiences of life. I sincerely desire to pass on important truths from me to my children and grandchildren. I'm writing these lessons in a manner suitable for sharing with my kids while driving together in the car, playing together at a park, or perhaps even sitting around the dinner table. I want to share these truths because I love God and I want my children, family and friends to love God and enjoy the blessings that come from walking in His ways.

One of the most important commands God has given to parents is recorded in Deuteronomy 6:5-7. "*Love the LORD your God with all your heart and with all your soul and with all your strength. These commandments that I give you today are to be upon your hearts. Impress them on your children. Talk about them when you sit at home and when you walk along the road, when you lie down and when you get up*" (NIV).

In this book I will make learning about personal finance as practical, biblically based, real, and interesting as possible by using anecdotes from my time in the Marines, and police work.

I will also show you:

- ✓ The importance of financial freedom and how to find it.
- ✓ The importance of staying away from debt and how to attack debt.
- ✓ Biblical views on finance.
- ✓ How and why we paid off our home and became completely debt free at the age of 37.
- ✓ How to conquer spending.
- ✓ The importance of a budget.
- ✓ Examples and strategies of living below your means.
- ✓ How much owning a vehicle can actually cost you.
- ✓ The importance of being grateful.
- ✓ Mortgage and home-buying advice.
- ✓ Dynasties.
- ✓ Explanation of assets, liabilities, and net worth.
- ✓ Investing made simple.
- ✓ Importance of being prepared financially for what life throws you – life insurance and rainy-day funds.
- ✓ Examples of servants and the magnitude of influence they can have on society.
- ✓ Career advice and the importance of an income, or multiple incomes.
- ✓ Explanation and examples of stewardship.
- ✓ Financial advice for vacations.
- ✓ Financial advice on food and beverage spending.

I will also highlight and provide examples of valuable leadership characteristics for business owners, recruiters and team members in charge of hiring.

TABLE OF CONTENTS

CHAPTER 1

DEBT AND FREEDOM

He looked me square in the eye with a puzzled look on his face and responded, "No way, this is as close to heaven on earth as it gets."

One of my most profound memories as a young child was hearing my mother crying behind a closed door. When I asked what was wrong, she said shamefully that she wrote a check they didn't have the money for. It hurt me deeply to see my mother cry like that, and it made a lasting impression on me. I can still feel my emotions from that day. That is the *result* of living paycheck to paycheck. If I can help it, this will never happen to my family. My hope is to help other families avoid this horrible situation.

I now understand why my dad did a great job teaching me how to stay out of debt. Every time I mentioned money, he interrupted with a sense of urgency, warning me, "Nate, get rid of those college loans before you do anything." His stern advice was heeded, and he supported our decision to pay off our house early. My dad encouraged us with words like, "Awesome" – "Good job" – and "Keep up the good work."

I read an interesting article in Fox Business by Ann Schmidt, entitled, *Many Americans run out of money before payday*. It stated almost a third of Americans run out of money before their next paycheck. With numbers that high, it is no surprise that 42% of

American workers experience more stress over their finances than in their relationships, career, or health. What was surprising is the article revealed that financial stress from running out of money before payday happens across all income levels. The survey stated this happens regularly to 32% of workers. Forty six percent of workers who carry over their credit card balance have more than $3,000 on their cards. According to the survey, the average interest rate on all U.S. credit cards is 21.44% and thousands of people are only paying off the interest each month. But many can't even manage that.

In my experience the biggest excuse used by people comfortable with debt is the philosophy, "You only live once." They rationalize "the right" to splurge and overspend because, "I work hard, and I deserve it. I've earned the right to a little treat." Many people think nothing of going into debt for a new vehicle, a house they can't afford, or a "well-deserved" vacation. It's true that we only live once in these bodies on the earth as it is now [see Revelation 21:1-4], which is why I say, "Don't mess it up!" The four stats presented in the article don't reflect the kind of living I want.

People in America are blessed to have choices about how they want to live, which is a good thing. My choice is to win and enjoy financial freedom with my family. I value freedom and try not to take it for granted. Many people living in the "land of the free" are in bondage to their debt. Once people experience financial freedom, they'll hopefully gain a better understanding of its benefits. If you are a person who has earthly freedoms, be thankful and give thanks, not to forget others who aren't as fortunate as you. Here are a couple of stories from my time in Iraq demonstrating how important freedom is.

On one particular mission in Iraq, while dismounted from our vehicles to provide security for a meeting with the Battalion commander, I was approached by a giddy and glowing Iraqi police officer who was looking around to see if anyone else was watching us. After confirming no one was looking, he took his wallet out and showed me a prayer card with a picture of Jesus on the cross. Then he pointed to it and gave me a thumbs up. It's sad that he had to hide his faith and love for Jesus because of fear of retribution, especially since that was one of the reasons we were there. I'm not talking about retribution in the form of ridicule or jabs that Christians are used to in America such as – "Look at that naive Christian." – "Where is your God now?" – "So why didn't God jump in and help you there?" etc. No, the retribution this Iraqi police officer might experience could quite literally cost him and his family their lives, just for the crime of being a Christian. The kind of retribution where you wake up to find your house on fire.

During our time In Iraq we used about five different Iraqi interpreters or "terps," and I got to know most of them to some extent. One of the terps grew up a Kurd in northern Iraq. Needless to say, he had no love lost for the former dictator and his regime. I never pressed him about what he saw or what was specifically done to him or his family. I do know he was old enough to see what happened on March 16, 1988. That was the date the Halabja Chemical Attack took place in the small Kurdish town of Halabja, Iraq, resulting in 3,200 to 5,000 Kurds being killed with another 7,000 to 10,000 injured from chemical burns.

The Halabja attack was the largest known chemical assault on a civilian population in the history of civilization. By my estimation this Kurdish Terp was approximately 20 to 30 years old at the time. The Supreme Iraqi Criminal Tribunal officially declared the Anfal campaign to have been a genocide against the Kurdish people. Kurdish officials estimated this genocide resulted in up to 182,000 Kurd deaths (us.gov.krd. Kurdistan Regional Government). During this same Anfal, 90% of the Kurdish villages and more than 20 small towns and cities were completely destroyed at the hands of the Ba'ath Regime.

Prior to leaving Iraq, this Kurdish Terp gave everyone in our platoon generous gifts to show his gratitude for what we did to liberate his people.

He hugged us genuinely and teared up whenever he talked about how much he appreciated Americans and his newfound freedom. I never saw a grown man cry *genuine heartfelt tears* as readily as he did.

I believe he saw some extremely heinous acts that he will never be able to forget.

Another Terp who assisted us with translating was from the Baghdad area. He told me how one of Saddam's sons, I believe it was Uday, had his limo driver randomly cruise around the university area of Baghdad until a beautiful young woman caught his attention. He would order his driver to slow down then point out the window to the woman. Then, at the snap of his finger, his men got out of the car and took her to see this tyrant. The same Terp said, "You thought Saddam was bad, but his sons had a reputation for being far worse."

Another incident that sticks out to me while serving in Iraq was the time a car with four Iraqi women drove up to me while our convoy was stopped. We were in a rural desert area and it was extremely rare to see women driving, let alone a car full of them. I was dismounted and in charge of ensuring all approaching vehicles stopped well over a hundred meters from our convoy. As they approached, I could see they were laughing and acting giddy, which I found odd since most women weren't allowed to drive. My suspicion quickly left as I could tell the young women were most likely meeting their first American Marine.

In Iraq, being a Marine was a big deal. Our military would intercept intel from the enemy whenever there was a change of battalions. The enemy's main concern was trying to figure out if the new unit was a Marine unit or another branch of the military. This esteem must have made its way to the civilian population as well. I tried to tell the girls to turn around and go the other way, but even if they spoke English, they weren't listening to a word I said. They had no intention of leaving. Instead, as they drove up they were reaching out of their windows trying to touch my face, all while smiling and giggling. My only job was to make sure they didn't go any further towards our convoy. They made no effort to do so, but they were determined to see a Marine up close. These poor girls obviously didn't get out much. I could only imagine what would have happened to them if their freedom adventure had been discovered.

Because of the culture training we received prior to going overseas, this incident made sense to me. It was stressed to us over and over that Iraqi culture treats their women much differently than we do in America. In the area we were deploying to, it was customary for the women to work long hours in the fields. We were told it would be common to see women carrying heavy baskets full of produce with their husbands most likely walking behind them empty handed.

This is an affront to us in America and our natural inclination would be to offer to help her carry the heavy load. But we were warned how important it was, even though we might want to be gentlemen, that we not step in or offer to assist because the Iraqi men would get furious at us for having any kind of contact with their women. It was frustrating to see this firsthand; women bent over all day tending to the fields or carrying heavy baskets down the road. Literally, the only thing we could do was be thankful for the many freedoms we had.

Another lesson I learned about freedom came while working my beat as a police officer. My partner for the day and I assisted a female motorist with a flat tire. Shortly afterwards, her husband arrived to help her and we were all soon enjoying a pleasant conversation while waiting for the tow truck. It turns out he was from Afghanistan and came to America around September 11, 2001. He explained how he left Afghanistan because it had become too dangerous and he wanted to find a better way of life. He told me about a family member who was a teacher at a university in Kabul and went missing. He believed the Taliban most likely kidnapped, imprisoned or killed him because his teaching style was not in line with their radical beliefs.

Within a couple years of coming to America he learned to speak English fluently. He landed a job selling natural gas door to door while learning the ins and outs of the company. Being really good at his job and knowing he could do it on his own, he soon started his own successful company based on hard work and his drive to succeed. I noticed they both drove very expensive BMWs and lived in an upscale neighborhood in one of Illinois' wealthiest suburbs. They appeared to be doing quite well.

I asked if he missed his homeland of Afghanistan. He paused in confusion, looked me square in the eye with a puzzled look on his face and said, "No way, this as close to heaven on earth as it gets." Hopefully, I've highlighted why freedom is a good thing. The same idea applies to financial freedom.

Being completely out of debt, I can comfortably use my vacation and holiday time. At work I have the option to sell my holiday and vacation time for money or use it for time off. Once I save enough cash, we can buy my first rental property if we so choose. My wife can continue to stay home with the kids, which is both of our dreams. Financial freedom can open the door to starting a business or taking a dream job you normally wouldn't be able to take. These are all options, which in my world I call freedoms.

Look at what we can learn from the Apostle Paul's words. In Acts 20:33-34, he tells us, "*I have never coveted anyone's silver or gold or fine clothes. You know that these hands of mine have worked to supply my own needs and even the needs of those who were with me.*"

The notes in my NLT Life Application Study Bible do a good job explaining this verse. It says that Paul was satisfied with whatever he had, wherever he was, so long as he could do God's work. Examine your attitudes towards wealth and comfort. If you constantly find yourself focusing on what you don't have rather than what you do have, it's time to re-examine your priorities and put God's work first. Paul was a tentmaker, and he supported himself with his trade. Paul didn't work to be rich but to be *free* from being *dependent* on *anyone*.

With that in mind, take a look at Proverbs 22:7 which teaches us the simple truth that, "*The borrower is slave to the lender.*"

The word that stood out to me in that short but important verse was slave. You are not a "bad" person for having debt, in fact you are in good company. However, you won't be able to enjoy financial freedom to its fullest potential if you have debt. On top of that, by being in debt you are putting your family in a tight spot in many ways.

For example, if you live paycheck to paycheck, what happens if you get injured or fired? What happens if your local, state, or federal government decides to shut your business down, leaving the fate of your business or job, in the hands of politicians? Your input doesn't matter, and it's out of your control if your business is allowed to stay open or not.

What you can control is your finances. Prepare for the uncontrollable events in your life. The only thing you can do under these circumstances is be prepared and protect your family. They are relying on you. What happens if you also have credit card debt along with being underwater on your home? What is your plan then tough guy? A leading cause of divorce in America is money issues. Look at an athletic team which just won a championship. Rarely will you see griping or friction amongst the players. When you are winning everyone is happy. Nothing can go wrong. But when you are losing it is a completely different story. People decide to jump ship, turn their back on the team and quit. Molehills typically become gigantic mountains. Debt or money trouble typically does *not* enhance a marriage. Broken marriages can destroy people and families.

I am strongly encouraging you to THINK ahead. I won't ask or beg you to do anything in this book. Take it or leave it. I believe you have free will, but I hope you will use that free will in a way that is in harmony with God's will and beneficial to your financial health, and His people. With that said, don't take your freedoms for granted or forget what the Creator *commands* of *freedom.* 1 Peter 2:16, "*For you are free, yet you are God's slaves, so don't use your freedom as an excuse to do evil.*" My goal is help you to create freedom for *good*, not to justify all too often abused earthly freedoms.

In closing, take a look at a strategy that has proven successful for centuries: The Mission of a Marine Corps Rifle Squad. "Locate, close with, and destroy the enemy by fire and maneuver, or to repel the enemy assault by fire and close combat." My financial suggestion to you would be: Locate (identify the financial problem) - close with (change your mindset, have a plan and move to execute the plan), destroy debt by training and execution, (financial freedom).

If you want financial freedom you have to fight for it.

CHAPTER 2

MINDSET

In the previous chapter, I explained why being in debt gives you less freedom over your life. In this chapter I will discuss practical ways to get out of debt and stay out of debt. The first step is changing your mindset on debt.

Let's face it, life is not easy. In America, we live in a society that makes it extremely easy to get into debt. Staying out of debt is a mindset you have to adopt and believe in, knowing you are going against the grain adopted by nearly everyone you know. One thing that helped my mindset was when I honestly separated "needs" from "wants." I learned the truth of this statement from my beautiful wife. Most of my "wants" in life are free. I want my kids to be Christians, productive citizens, and happy.

Just as important as understanding the drawbacks of debt is making the decision to change your behavior. Make good financial decisions. Don't fall into the trap of instant gratification from consumer goods that you will quickly grow tired of. People who constantly have trucks delivering packages to their front door from shopping online are seeking fulfillment in an unproductive way. Don't rely on needing a package at your door to make your day.

Christmas was an interesting day for me as a kid. I had all these new toys, clothes, and other material goods I just opened. I should've been really happy, right? But that wasn't always the case. Instead, after a few hours I found myself counting the days until the next Christmas and seeking more. Honestly, most of the toys were somewhat boring by noon. I suspect this must be true for adult consumers too. Changing your mindset might not be an instantaneous change but more like putting together a puzzle, one small piece at a time. You'll never finish without putting the first piece in place.

Another frame of mind that helped me was learning to be confident with who I am. God made us exactly the way he wanted, physically, emotionally, and mentally. The sooner you can accept that, or understand something you don't like, the sooner you'll be over it. I try not to care what other people think about me all that much. Instead, I care about what God thinks about me.

That hasn't always been the case. Confidence is something that comes with small victories, like completing a successful plan or gaining experience.

My friends at work are constantly teasing me about the car I drive. They say, "Well at least I have air conditioning in my car." I give them a confident smile and paint them a picture of what policing will feel like when they are 65 years old. A look of panic consumes their face. Confidence allows me to avoid expensive vehicle purchases and helps me stay out of debt.

Confidence is something that you develop and nurture. After graduating from college without having a job lined up, I felt worthless. During college, I worked part-time at a hotel. This was never intended to be my career, but I was productive and employed. I left being productive behind and came home with no plan.

I decided to enlist in the United States Marine Corps, which changed my life. I cannot begin to tell you how much of a positive effect this organization had on me and my family. It shaped who I am today. I would not trade my Eagle Globe and Anchor that I earned or any of the brotherhood gained in the Marines for all the money in the world. The crazy thing is, the Marine Corps paid me for all these great lessons. Conversely, college left me in debt. Am I saying college isn't a good option? Not at all, education is extremely important. It does depend on the person and what occupation they are seeking, and how much they are willing to put into it. Unfortunately, and something I wish I could do over, I attended college strictly for the degree and not necessarily to learn.

In college I learned a lot about life and being on my own. I learned about going to class and completing my assigned work, even when I failed to give it my best effort. At times I would expend more effort messing with spacing, font size and margins to meet the minimum page requirements than I did in researching the paper. I actually turned papers in a page short. I never got a hundred on the papers, but I never failed them either. Looking back, I wish one of my teachers would have given me a zero just to teach me a lesson. I can't believe I used to think an 80 or 85 percent grade was okay. Anything less than 100 percent in the Marines won't cut it. If any of my Drill Instructors saw me only giving 80 percent effort, I would pay for it. We're all guilty of this at times, but it pays to improve your effort. A hardworking mindset is important, seek it.

Immediately upon our arrival at boot camp, after standing on the yellow footprints for some time we were issued our gear. It was our basic survival gear, and it all fit in a small footlocker. In fact, when we arrived at MCRD San Diego all we needed were the clothes on our back and some form of ID. When you got there, they boxed up all your personal possessions and you were provided with shelter, uniforms, water, and chow.

For most of boot camp, shelter and chow were not readily available. We appreciated the days when you actually got to finish your meal, which I could count on one hand. We weren't starving, but I think we were close. I went down to 135 pounds at one point. It was demoralizing to hear your Drill Instructor say, "Stop eating, you are done," after only wolfing down half your chow. That was the worst command in boot camp. Our instructions were to stop chewing that very instant, spit out whatever you had in your mouth and turn your cup upside down on your tray, dousing that delicious uneaten chow. Everything was done for a reason, even if we didn't know what that reason was. In times of war, you might go days without eating and you needed to know that you can do it again.

During boot camp I was sick two different times. The first time was likely walking pneumonia, or what the drill instructors called the "recruit crud." That first month it seemed as if everyone in my platoon was sick. I developed similar, but even more severe respiratory symptoms later in bootcamp. Going on "humps" and three mile runs with the recruit crud was pure torture. I remember coughing and spitting out phlegm that was pure blood. I had to fight to keep myself upright and ignore the illness.

If I had gone to sick bay or passed out, I would've been held back to the next platoon. Typically, there is another company exactly one week behind you. Unfortunately for me, my platoon, Golf Company, was two weeks ahead of the next platoon, Kilo Company. Two more weeks in boot camp would feel like two years. Kilo Company was my enemy, and I couldn't let him catch me. Or, if you were sick for an extended period of time you might even get recycled where they started your training all over again from scratch. No thanks.

I kept going because I couldn't wait to see my family on graduation day, and my goal was to be a Marine. Mentally, I refused to fail. Make goals, fight for what motivates you and don't stop until you reach that goal.

To help plan your goal, the Marine Corps has the answer. We have what is known as the Six Troop Leading Steps, or the acronym BAMCIS

B egin the planning (Write out your goals and desired timetable)

A rrange the reconnaissance (Figure out how to research what you need to do to accomplish your goal)

M ake the reconnaissance (Do the research)

C omplete the plan (Get specific with how you are going to fulfill your goal)

I ssue the order (Actually put everything into practice)

S upervise (Make sure you are disciplined enough to stick with the plan)

It's amazing what you can do when you really *want* something bad enough, like cutting out cable or satellite TV, driving a modest car, or downsizing your home to get out of debt. It hurts at first, but you can get used to it. We cut cable 7 years ago and it hurt, but now I don't miss it at all. I can't believe I *actually* paid for all that garbage.

My dad always said money can't buy happiness. As a kid I didn't believe him, but I agree with him now. When my mom and firstborn son were in the hospital, it wouldn't have mattered to me if I was a billionaire (My mother spent about one month in the hospital gravely ill, and my oldest son spent the first two months of his life in the NICU), I would have traded it all for spending time with my family and praying for them to get well.

On the other hand, it would have mattered if I were in debt up to my eyeballs trying to pay all the bills from my son's hospital room. Just another stressor to worry about when your world is falling apart. Have an emergency backup. Since I had vacation time and money saved, I was able to take seven weeks off. At my job, if you work overtime you can either take the overtime for pay or save it for time off. The most you could save was 480 hours, and I had right around that, which is 60 days off. I didn't blow through my vacation time as soon as I got it, I saved it for a rainy day. In my family's case, it was a rainy two months.

You can *change* if you *want* to. I changed my behaviors, habits, and mindset numerous times, but I was only *successful* in changing when I really wanted it bad enough. Sometimes you will have to make some hard decisions or go through something grueling, but it will grow you mentally. *Changing* your *core mindset* can be *very powerful*.

If you want to stay away from debt you can. Make smart decisions and change your mindset. Don't be a super consumer, develop confidence, and save for a rainy day. It's important to plan for the future and not just live for the moment.

Have you asked God for help in changing any behaviors, mindsets, or habits in your life? Just ask, you never know.

CHAPTER 3

SPENDING

Ninety-three times. I could be off by a couple, but that is the number of times I counted the words fool, foolish, or foolishness in the book of Proverbs. While not considered polite to use today, the word fool is very important when discussing finances. Look at Proverbs 21:20, "*The wise have wealth and luxury, but fools spend whatever they get.*" That passage speaks for itself and needs no interpretation. If you're spending more than you're earning, especially on things you don't need, you're a *fool*. This type of spending leads to debt, which (hopefully) we agree is bad. Spending more than you earn is negligent and will certainly lead to preventable stress within your life and relationships. Debt prevents you from *prospering*, and God is rooting for us to prosper; I have no doubt about that.

The best way to take control of your spending is to plan and stick to a budget. Sit down and look at everything you've spent money on in the last six months. Break your spending down into needs and wants. Make sure you write everything down, accounting for literally every penny. Look at how much you spend on your needs. When you do, you will usually be shocked at how much of your money is going to things like this. Look at what you are spending on wants. The numbers may be shocking, which is exactly why it *needs* to be written down and *dissected*.

Could you do better in a specific area? For example, consider the money spent on cable or satellite TV. Is this really a need? Some people are so involved in TV and shows, they have come to *believe* it is a need, but it isn't. I used to be one of those people. It didn't take long to realize it *wasn't* a need. I estimate we saved at least $4,000 over the last six years. If you were to apply that $4,000 to paying off debt or your mortgage principle, that's what I would call a huge *win*.

Without a doubt, spending is something you can readily improve on. I have seen firsthand what overspending leads to. I've seen how government agencies spend "their" money. Why are leaders of families spending like we are government leaders who are able to print money? Financial expert Dave Ramsey is fond of saying, "You're spending like you're in Congress." Family leaders, let's not emulate anything Congress does, especially when it comes to spending. Unlike them, you don't have your own printing press.

I talked about the importance of winning with money, but it's equally important to learn how to avoid losing with money. Out of control spending is losing. Spending too much on your wants is losing. Spending too much for junk you want is beyond losing, you're being demolished. It has been said, "We spend money on things we can't afford, to buy things we don't need, to impress people we don't even like."

If you habitually spend your money buying anything at convenience stores or gas stations other than fuel, you are losing. The mark-up on those items is insane. Gas stations make very little money selling you gas. Instead, they make their money on all the junk for sale inside. Think about that. They make most of their profit, overhead, employees' salaries, and expenses on what you buy inside. I know this can be hard, but it's called a "convenience store" for a reason. Don't go inside and buy their junk.

Serving in Iraq, I became used to having unlimited access to Gatorade, water, and energy drinks; all provided to us at no cost, courtesy of our Uncle Sam. Iraq is a desert climate and it was scorching hot for most of our deployment. With our heavy gear, it was a constant battle to stay hydrated, so these things really were somewhat of a need versus a want.

I learned to love being hydrated, and l took this love home with me. Whenever I stopped at a gas station, I instinctively found myself buying a couple Gatorades, sometimes accompanied by a snack food or dessert item. Before you knew it, I was paying seven bucks and change for junk.

In case you didn't know, Gatorade is full of sugar. It isn't good for you. I eventually realized this was too expensive and I could do better, so I began buying in bulk at the grocery store. I could get 12 Gatorades for the price of two in the gas station. That is an amazing amount of savings. Since it was expensive and unhealthy, I eventually stopped drinking Gatorade and now stay hydrated with water, which is a lot cheaper and much better for you.

I've never bought a lottery ticket on my own, but I will admit to participating in lottery office pools here and there. The only reason I bought-in was I couldn't imagine sitting in a room with 17 empty desks. Coworkers are what make work enjoyable, so I assumed five dollars was worth it. My assumption about lotteries has since changed. I could go through the numbers and recite statistics about the chances of you winning the lottery, but that would be a waste of time. I'll just go ahead and say it. If you are reading this book, you will not win the lottery. It's that simple. You might as well consider it a donation to the government. If I was your financial advisor, I would tell you to save the money you normally spend on lottery tickets and place it in a decent performing index or mutual fund. I know that doesn't sound exciting, but playing the lottery is stupid. Let's try to stay away from stupid.

One of my favorite quotes is from an Army General when he was speaking to the media about logistics from an approaching hurricane. They continued asking questions that ran in circles. He reminded them a couple times, "Don't get stuck on stupid, reporters," but they didn't seem to take the hint. When a particular reporter asked the same question, he finally had enough. He pointed at the reporter excitedly and replied, "You are stuck on stupid, I'm not going to answer that question." We all have our moments, but the goal is to not get stuck on stupid.

A few years ago an officer in my unit identified a possible suspect in a series of armed robberies. We planned to put the suspect under surveillance and catch him in the act. Just as we were sitting down for our operational briefing, a call came in alerting us to another armed robbery that fit the M.O. and description of our suspect. We had no doubt this was our guy so we raced to intercept him.

One of the officers located him driving about 10 blocks from his apartment. When he went to pull him over, the suspect refused to stop and a high-speed chase ensued. My partner and I were wearing plainclothes when we immediately took off toward his apartment, thinking he would head there. The suspect ditched his car in a convenience store parking lot around the corner from his apartment then ran right toward us. I was able to chase after him, causing him to run directly back towards the numerous squad cars that were originally pursuing him. Needless to say, we were able to arrest him after a *very* short foot pursuit.

I later learned video of the bad guy was captured by a surveillance camera as he tried making his way back to his apartment. One of my coworkers captured a still photograph from the footage and sent it to the guys in my unit just to bust my chops. I was chasing the bad guy in plainclothes with my pistol out. I was sighting in on the armed offender while having an interesting gait (in all fairness it is very hard to do). The joke was, I looked like the angry manger from the fast food place trying to get his money back, since I didn't necessarily look like a cop. Luckily, it all ended without anyone getting hurt. My physical features and appearance were very similar to the bad guy and the two of us also happened to be dressed alike. I could've easily been mistaken for him by the large number of responding officers, and that would not have ended well.

I later noticed the background of the photo had advertising signs for lottery tickets, Gatorade, and other junk food items posted outside the convenience store. Inside you will find nothing but junk. Lottery tickets, cheap cigars, tobacco, junk food, candy, alcohol, energy drinks, various trinkets, and Gatorade. These ads deliberately target people who have yet to master their spending habits. I say that because all these items have huge markups and are completely overpriced. A 20 oz. soda will cost you around $2, this is more than what it would cost you to by a two-liter of the same soda at a grocery store. There are better ways in life to be smart with your purchases, and it is important to help people improve on their spending habits.

According to millionairefoundry.com, most millionaires believe gambling is a waste of money with 74 percent spending $0 on gambling in the previous year. If your goal is to improve on spending, ask yourself what your long term wants and needs are. My long term wants are the same as my needs. I want to retire, spend time with my family, and watch my kids play sports, and attend other school events. This is also my need. I *need* to be at those games. My kids *need* me at those games. I need to be at their graduation. I *need* to play catch with them. I need to be able to take them to college, and they need me to be there as well.

If you rein in your spending now, it will only help your chances of enjoying family needs in the future. I'll have to work in some form, and quite honestly, I'll want to work in some form for most of my life; but if I can control my spending, this will help me do something I truly enjoy, regardless of the salary.

In boot camp we had a Senior Drill Instructor. Like the name suggests, he was the head drill instructor of our platoon and he was distinguished by wearing a black belt. The other four drill instructors reported to and took orders from him. He was our father figure and treated us "slightly" better than the other drill instructors. I will never forget his famous saying whenever we messed up. "Are you out of your *@&# mind!" or "You have lost your #*$@&*# mind." He would inch closer to your face as he bellowed with spit mist landing on your face, eyes, and lips.

Everything was done for a reason. He was the perfect example of a drill instructor. Tall, muscular, and mean looking. When he said something, it was usually with eyes bulging out of his sockets, saliva flying, while veins and muscles protruded from his neck. His voice bellowed off the walls of the squad bay. When he got mad—stand by.

When he smoked us, it meant we really messed up. Being smoked is a term for taking recruits to the dirt or the pit and giving us extra training. He made us move into platoon formation, barking orders. His expression said it all. He was so disappointed and enraged his eyes literally looked as if he was seeing red. He reigned over us, standing tall on a platform at the head of the formation with his arms crossed. We would switch from pushups, to burpees, to mountain climbers in a moment's notice at the very instant the new order left his mouth. Sometimes we wouldn't even have time to go from the push-up to the burpee position before the next order came out. All random movements were undertaken with a speed and intensity that created an enormous dust cloud from 50 recruits moving at lightning speed, kicking the dirt with each new command. This cloud of dust made it hard to breathe and added to our misery.

When we finally survived our thrashing, we looked as though we had just came through an intense dust storm. The dirt stuck fast to our sweaty faces. I will never forget the taste of that San Diego dirt and sandy grit in my teeth. If we were really lucky, another drill instructor would run around, "accidentally" kicking up dirt and sand as we received our punishment.

The crazy part is our senior drill instructor wasn't the scariest of our drill instructors. However, if he was the one smoking us, it was bad. He was the drill instructor who treated us the best, making his disappointment hurt the most, mentally and physically. Mentally because we felt we let him down, and physically because it was usually more intense and longer than your normal quick thrashing.

The saying from my Senior Drill Instructor might not mean a lot to you, but it had quite the impact on me. I will use it as a teaching moment.

If you spend more than you make, if you buy a vehicle for $45,000 when you make $50,000 a year, if you drive the same type of car as your doctor but only make a third of what he/she makes then you are "out of your @$^%$# mind." I feel as if I work at a doctor's office when I pull into the parking lot at work. I'm surrounded by a plethora of luxury cars.

But to be honest, you will find that same scene everywhere in "middle class" America these days. If you make purchases based on if you "think" you can afford the payment, you have indeed lost your @@#@$ mind. If you spend based on emotions, only focusing on the short term, you have not only lost your @#$@#$$%%%^% mind, you need to grow up and find a solution to the underlying problem. You owe that much to yourself and your family. I can assure you, being a consumer will not make you happy. If that was the solution to happiness, why do people constantly buy more and more? If you are happy with your new shiny vehicle, why are you trading it in after six months?

One of my middle school teachers, a Vietnam Marine Veteran, once told me this: "If that kid had an idea, it would roll around his head like a BB in a box car." He wasn't referring to this kid's grades, he was talking about the young man's lack of common sense and decision-making skills. Don't be the guy with a BB rolling around in your head. Common sense and basic math apply to spending. Don't spend more than you make. Get on a budget.

In the Marines we used to go on humps. A hump was a hike with a large heavy pack that we carried on our backs called a "main pack" that was loaded and stuffed with all our gear. I would estimate it easily weighed over 60 pounds. Along with our packs, we also had our flak-jacket, rifle, and Kevlar helmet, which easily added another 15 pounds or more. During these humps we went up and down mountains at distances of over 10 miles. In boot camp we all packed the same gear--uniformity is everything in boot camp.

After graduating boot camp, humps and training evolutions in the field were completely different. For the most part, we were responsible for bringing what we needed. If you didn't pack your cold weather gear, you were going to freeze at night. You were free to bring your own protein bars or trail mix, but yours truly had to lug it around because all these things added weight to the pack, you only brought along the absolute bare necessities. A saying you hear a lot in the Marines is - ounces equal pounds, pounds equal pain. My experience in the field helped me realize how little humans actually need to survive. We could live in the field for days and survive on just what was on our back. Conversely, many people rent storage lockers to store their extra toys and junk they have accumulated. Three car garages are not big enough for all the junk we possess, which puts things in perspective. You don't "need" as much stuff as you think you do, you just "want" it.

Here is an example of planning ahead to save money. A few years ago, I flew to Florida for one of my Marine brother's wedding. I had breakfast at home and left my house around 10 am on a Thursday and would be gone for the next two and a half days. I took advantage of free snacks on the plane for lunch. After arriving in Florida around 4 pm, I checked into the hotel. After changing I went straight to the welcome party. I noticed the invitation said there would be hors d'oeuvres and appetizers served. I learned "hors d'oeuvres" actually meant "free dinner."

At the welcoming party, the hosts provided goodie bags with sunscreen, small gifts, and trail mix. Lucky me, lunch the following day would be trail mix; perfect for my day at the beach. In the morning I took advantage of the free continental breakfast at the hotel. I supplemented my trail mix lunch with a banana and peanut butter packets from the breakfast buffet. The wedding was in the evening and dinner was served afterwards. The next morning, you guessed it, another free continental breakfast. I brought a banana and peanut butter packets for my final lunch at the airport. I was away from my house for seven meals and never paid one cent for food.

Use what is available, plan ahead, and control your spending. This will prevent you from throwing your hard-earned money away.

CHAPTER 4

DYNASTY AND WINNING

I mentioned earlier how important winning is. Winning involves preparation, training, learning (coached and self-taught), trial and error, resilience--the list goes on. Winning leads to championships, and championships lead to dynasties. This concept can also be applied to finances. Deciding to pass on purchasing a "want" you don't really need, getting out of debt, or being wise with your next vehicle purchase are all examples of winning. If you make wise financial decisions, you should have many wins under your belt. But you have to commit if you wish to create a dynasty. Dynasties take time, but it will happen if you are patient and make smart choices.

I'll use an example in my life to highlight some of these points. This example has wants and needs, maturity, wisdom, evil wives, and expensive vehicles, all wrapped into one.

The second car I owned was a vehicle I bought from my brother. He took excellent care of it and sold it to me for a fair price after he left for college. I was about seventeen years old and my lack of maturity really showed with this purchase. I spent all the money I had saved on that car. Could you imagine spending your entire net worth on a car now? I hope not, but some people do.

Because it took all my money, I ended up neglecting all the normal routine maintenance and repairs. It wasn't long before the brakes and rotors were beyond gone, and I had worn the tires bald. Luckily, I was going to college soon, so I stored it in the garage.

A decade later, something happened that changed my life forever. I got married and my beautiful wife moved in. I envisioned restoring and fixing my antique car, but my wife saw things a little differently. The car was taking up much needed garage space, and she knew it hadn't been running for over a decade. My wife gave me the option, but she said it in such a way it made me think twice about restoring my classic car, "You know, we could really use the extra space in the garage. What do you plan on doing with that car?" I confirmed her fear. I told her I planned on restoring it. Confused, she said, "If you want to restore that car, that sounds great. But if you don't do it soon, please get rid of it."

I did some research into what it would realistically cost to fix the brakes and rotors, replace the tires, exhaust, fuel pump, battery, chrome repair, and transport it to a mechanic. If I did all these things and got it running, I would be paying for extra car insurance.

I realized having a second car was a want, not a need. Why would I pay so much for a want? I had done fine without it for over a decade. I estimated the work might cost as much as $2,500--possibly more. It pains me to say it, but she was right. I decided to sell it and posted it online for $1,000. I was honest and explained everything that was wrong with it. To my surprise, within five minutes I had two calls and an hour later my dreams were crushed.

Luckily, my wife waited until after we were married to bring up the car or the big day might never have materialized. Never to be underestimated, I know why she didn't mention the car until we were officially hitched. She dedicated a lot of time, thought, and resources in her victorious plot. I am sure this historic victory of hers gets brought up routinely during girls night. "Tell us about the time you shamed your husband into selling his car so you could have more room in the garage to sand and stain old furniture. That's my favorite story."

Being bummed about selling my car, I decided to turn the situation into a positive by applying extra money to my mortgage principal. I matched what I had gotten for the car and applied two grand to the next mortgage payment. This gave me peace of mind. Not only had I made money from something I hadn't used in over a decade, I didn't have to spend any extra money to get it fixed. I would say that was a $3,500-point swing in building our wealth--not to mention the debt we chipped away from our mortgage. It was a win, win, win (my wife was extremely happy with me for clearing out room in the garage).

Let's use the analogy of a pick 6 in football. Imagine your team is up by a score of 10 to 3. The other team is marching down the field--it looks like they are about to score. They are on your 5-yard line when one of your players intercepts the football and runs 95 yards the other way to score 6 points (hence the pick 6). Prior to the pick, the score was 10 to 3 with your team winning. The chances of the other team scoring were very high as they were about to score 6 with a TD and one for an extra point, for a total of 7 points. The score could very easily have been a 10 to 10--tie ball game.

Instead, your team just scored the pick 6 and added the extra point for a total of 7 points. The score is now 17 to 3 and your team is in a comfortable lead, having all the momentum. All you need to do to win is stick with your game plan. The pick 6 was one small act that most likely won the game for your team, one big *win*. Keep accomplishing small game changing acts like that and you will eventually have tons of wins under your belt, more championships, and a well-built dynasty.

Winning is contagious.

CHAPTER 5

MY SECOND STRONGEST BELIEF: FAMILY

"The righteous One knows what is going on in the home of the wicked, He will bring disaster on them." (Proverbs 21:12)

Make a list of people who had an influence on your life. How many of them influenced you positively? Would anyone put criminals and gang members on their list? Such a list might look like this: My uncle showed me how to hustle and sell drugs. I watched my mother get abused by the various guys she invited into her house. I watched my mom use drugs. I never got love from my mom or dad. I was never really loved by anyone, including my family. I never met my dad/mom. My mom told me to go shoplift for her because I was too young to get arrested.

What kind of an influence are you having on your family, friends, and coworkers?

Deuteronomy 6:6-7 gives us the following instructions, *"And you must commit yourselves wholeheartedly to these commands that I am giving you today. Repeat them again and again to your children. Talk about them when you are at home and when you are on the road, when you are going to bed and when you are getting up."*

Fathers, do you make time to talk to your children about God? Did future gang members and criminals get a bedtime story and pray with their parents before bed? My guess would be no. I have noticed that most criminals seldom have positive interactions with their family. Deadbeat parents can be found in all economic strata, and this must change if we are to return to being a great nation.

In many situations, the parent is more unlikeable than the 15 or 16-year-old criminal. "That poor kid has no chance," is a phrase every police officer has uttered. We say it to each other and under our breath after leaving a filthy home with bare mattresses on the floor, rampant bugs or other infestations, and signs of either alcohol or drug abuse by the parent(s). If only these parents would do an internal audit of how their actions and behaviors were affecting their kids, what a difference it would make.

Should teachers, media, pop culture, government, and nannies be the ones raising our kids? Or should parents be teaching their kids? Hopefully, most would agree that the answer should be parents. Proverbs 1:8 says, "*Listen, my son, to your father's instruction and do not forsake your mother's teaching.*" Would you say loving parents help mold a good kid? Yes, I think you would. Do I have to say it? Look at the bad people in the world, now look at their parent(s). I realize there are people out there who were raised in a loving home and then went on to live a life of crime, but I rarely run into that.

Exodus 20:2-6 records God talking to the Israelites after leading them from slavery in Egypt. He took them to Mt. Sinai where they formed a new nation. The passage immediately takes off with the strong declaration, "*I am the Lord your God... I lay the sins of the parents upon their children; the entire family is affected - even children in the third and fourth generation of those who reject me. But I lavish unfailing love for a thousand generations on those who love me and obey my commands.*"

Listen up parents. Your faith and behavior not only affect you, it determines the future fate of your family for generations to come. All too often, infamous last names in my town tell a story of whom I am dealing with. The phrase the apple doesn't fall far from the tree is a sad truism.

Living in poverty isn't a great place to be. One might ask, "Why is poverty present?" In America, I believe a lot of it boils down to what God told the Israelites 3,000 years ago. Bad decisions (sin) and turning your back on God usually lead to bad results. I can't stress this enough. Show me a place with high crime and violence, and you will usually find a lack of love, leadership, and guidance from parent(s).

If you want a recipe for poverty and pain, here it is:

According to the U.S. Census Bureau, children living in father-absent homes are nearly four times more likely to live in poverty. Additionally, 44% of children raised by a single mother live in poverty. By contrast, just 12 % of children in married-couple families were living in poverty. In the United States the median income for a household with a single mother is $35,400, but for a home with a married couple, the median income is $85,300.

According to the U.S. Department of Justice, 7 out of 10 youth housed in state-operated correctional facilities, including detention and residential treatment, come from fatherless homes. Living in a fatherless home is a major contributing factor in substance abuse, with children from such homes accounting for 75% of all adolescent patients currently being treated in substance abuse centers. Eighty-five percent of all children exhibiting some type of behavioral disorder come from a fatherless home, while 63% of youth suicides were living in a fatherless home when they made their fateful decision.

According to the National Principals Association Report: 71% of all high school dropouts come from fatherless homes, nine times the national average. The U.S. Department of Health and Human Services reports that 71% of pregnant teenagers lack a father.

Children from fatherless homes are 20 times more likely to end up incarcerated. Anger breeds and grows ferociously with a lack of parental love. In my experience, personal anger rarely yields anything positive.

One "family" that sadly comes to mind was the absolute worst I ever saw during my law-enforcement career. We had a report that one of the kids was breaking into a car by the owner. "How dare that citizen confront me, luckily I am armed," this kid thought. Not only did the bad guy take valuables from the car, he also fired numerous shots at the car's owner to really teach him a lesson. "Don't get in my way."

This young man's household consisted of a single mom who birthed ten children from at least three different fathers. Knowing this family was causing a lot of trouble in the neighborhood, I decided to introduce myself to the mother. I was sure she was just "overwhelmed" with all these kids.

Unfortunately, that wasn't the case. I tried to give her a subtle hint that if her kids kept robbing people in the area, there was a strong possibility one of them would eventually get shot and killed. To this day, I can't explain her bizarre reaction to hearing what would have been a terrifying and sobering reality check to any normal mother. She didn't display an ounce of concern, far from it. Instead, she just broke out in a large grin, smiling. It was at this moment I realized this woman truly didn't care about anything.

Well, unfortunately, just like I predicted, someone finally got shot. Within a year of our conversation, her boyfriend, who was about half her age, was shot with his *own* gun while attempting to rob someone during an online robbery set-up. The boyfriend responded to a person who posted something for sale online and told him he wanted to buy it and recommended they meet up. The seller showed up with the item and the bad guy showed up with a gun and threatened the other person if he didn't give up what he was selling. Luckily, this time the good guy defended himself and didn't get hurt. The bad guy had a bad day. He got shot by his own gun, visited the hospital, and eventually went to jail.

This same family had nothing downstairs except a fridge and stove. They had no couch, no table, no furniture. When the kids were hungry, they would order a pizza or go to the corner store. They obtained their food by either stealing or buying an unhealthy snack food for dinner, it didn't matter either way to them.

Did their mother/father fail them? Yes, they did. Every individual is responsible for their own actions, but they didn't receive much help from the people who should help or correct their bad behavior.

I remember another time when our unit was watching a very bad guy. This perp had over 50 arrests on his record. At the time, he was suspected of having committed a series of burglaries and other crimes all over the city.

As a nice gesture, he would drop his girlfriend off at work for her midnight shift. But who was watching all the young children in the house while the two of them were gone? The kids were asleep, his girlfriend was at work, he had possession of her vehicle, and most of the rest of the people in the neighborhood were getting some well-deserved rest for their big day of work the next morning. Everything was working out perfectly for him. For the next few hours, he had complete freedom to commit his crimes with impunity. Although his girlfriend might not have an idea her boyfriend was living this double life, I still believe both the mom and the boyfriend were at fault. They both made bad decisions--she knew what type of guy he was.

You would be surprised how many people I run into who neglect to put their kids in car seats or if they do, they never buckle them in. When I pull them over and point out what they are doing, rather than thank me for pointing out how dangerous this is for their children, they act as if the whole thing is my fault. They give me a look that says, "Don't preach to me! Just do what you gotta do" (meaning just give me the ticket and let me go so I can get on with MY life).

In these cases, it was evident to me there was no love for their kids. I had one lady roll her eyes and ask me, "Well, are you going to buy me a car seat then?" Now it would be one thing if she truly was poor, but she was driving an expensive two or three-year old Jeep Grand Cherokee. She had money for the payments, but somehow she couldn't find an extra $50 in her budget to purchase a car seat that might save her child's life.

They say they love their kids, but I believe it's a lie. It's sad to watch. I would guess that most of those kids who don't get put in car seats will never grow up to be productive members of society. I am not saying this is because they weren't put in a car seat, rather it's indicative of being brought up without love and care.

A similar family comes to mind, but the major difference is this mom at least pretended to care when our investigation led to her son's arrest for robbing a corner store at gunpoint. We had this young man dead to rights. We recovered video surveillance footage clearly showing her son pointing a large revolver directly in the clerk's face. When I showed her a still image of her son robbing the store, unbelievably, she stated with absolute certainty and confidence that the man in the picture looked like her son. This surprised me because I am usually met with denials. I then asked if she recognized the distinct backpack that was also captured in the surveillance footage. She confirmed she did, in fact, recognize the backpack then promptly retrieved it from his room. This level of cooperation rarely happens.

The neighborhood was fed up with this family and were constantly complaining, asking me to do something. I reached out to the landlord and informed him of the problems in the area. I explained that this family was the worst of the worst, and sooner or later one of the sons living at this problem house was going to kill someone. The homeless shelter, which paid for their housing, finally agreed to relocate them to a better fit. Needless to say, within a year, one of them robbed, shot and killed someone over $200 worth of weed.

I see the same themes repeating themselves over and over, all too often. Fatherless homes, pregnant females smoking, drinking, and using drugs. Feral children outside at all times of the day and night to where the street life has now become and integral part of their lifestyle. Kids and babies left home alone. Kids as young as 8 saying, "F the police!" Mothers slapping their kid's hands if they try to wave to the police. Kids eating a bag of chips for dinner. Mothers who allow their children to skip school year-round. Kids as young as 10 selling drugs and holding guns for older brothers or uncles they look up to.

Marine Gunnery Sergeant R. Lee Ermey said it well in his book, *Gunny Rules*, "Management starts at home. Mom and dad are our first and most effective role models."

During the two months our newborn son was in the NICU, I noticed the majority of the other infants with him in the ward *never* had a visitor. No mother, father, grandma, or an aunt or uncle, nobody. Sadly, the need for visitors and affection for most of the NICU newborns was so great that community members volunteered to visit and hold all these unvisited children. While this is heartwarming and touching, these people were strangers. These young babies needed the love and warmth that only a mother and father can give.

While on the job, I responded to a disturbance call at one of our local bars. Upon arrival, we discovered a man we later learned was the bouncer, covered in blood. It looked like his shirt had been taken off and drenched in a pool of blood and then put back on. Other officers responding to the scene apprehended the bad guys before they could flee the area. Thank God, because the bouncer didn't know their names and they most likely would've gotten away with the crime.

The original "disturbance" call turned out to be an attempted murder. During our investigation we discovered our two bad guys were a father and 17-year-old son duo (It is very rare for a criminal to have any sort of relationship with their father like we will see in the next two anecdotes). Whenever we arrest a juvenile, by law we are required to get their parents' information and contact them as soon as possible. I wish I had kept a tally throughout the years of how few juveniles actually knew their father. I would estimate around 7 out of 10 juveniles we arrested never appeared to have any kind of a relationship with their father whatsoever.

The pair had been drinking and tried to enter the bar but the bouncer rightfully refused to allow the 17-year-old in. Not liking the bouncer's decision, the father pulled out a knife and stabbed him several times. What an example this man set for his teenage son. He just taught this young man that rules don't apply to them; and if someone tells us what we don't want to hear, it's okay to just go ahead and stab them to get what you want.

Needless to say, our department was quite familiar with the 17-year-old. Despite his young age, he was already involved in gangs and had a violent and extensive rap sheet. Are you surprised? For some reason, the father ended up at the hospital. I believe he cut his hand during the attack. I was in charge of watching him at the hospital. This man showed no remorse and never once asked how the person he stabbed was doing. All he could do was talk about himself. Most likely he saw himself as the victim. As you can imagine, he is already out of prison. But don't worry, I am sure he is back out there, mentoring his loved ones with his wonderful pearls of wisdom.

With that being said, is there such a thing as a perfect father? No. I'm not perfect, and I have no problem admitting that. Not even close. But I don't use that as an excuse to avoid trying to raise my kids the way God intended, and I love them very much. It is our job and obligation to lead by example and talk to them about how important our Christian walk is while on this earth.

Remember, disciplining your child is loving your child. According to the Bible, parents need to correct their children's behavior and teach them right from wrong. I am determined not to be the kind of parent who gets mad at the teacher for telling me my "Little Johnny did this today." My response won't be, "Not my little Johnny! He's an angel! I can promise you, the principal will be hearing about this." Truth can hurt, but it is important. And yes, they are kids. They will get into trouble. They have the same sinful nature of rebellion we all have. Job 5:7 says we are *"born unto trouble as the sparks fly upward."*

One day, our Sergeant called us all into the office and informed us that we had a secret detail to conduct. This mission was so hush hush, we weren't even given a hint what it was about. This was the first time in my career, and most likely the last, where we didn't have the complete details of an operation. All we knew was that our duty was to assist the FBI in executing a search warrant at a terrorism suspect's residence within our jurisdiction. We were given just enough information to accomplish our mission--which was mostly providing additional security and backup. After arriving and securing the residence, I spoke with an agent who provided me with some more details.

The FBI recently prevented an attack that would have killed hundreds of soldiers at a National Guard Armory in Joliet, Illinois. They had one of the suspected terrorists (Hasan) in custody at the airport. When I later read a Chicago Tribune article titled, *National Guard Member and Cousin Given Long Prison Terms For Terror Plot*, I learned Hasan was raised in a terrible environment. Hasan's lawyers claimed he was scarred by a terrible childhood filled with years of abuse.

The father was a gang member and drug addict. The abuse Hasan endured was so severe that his mother shot his father in the face after he tried forcing her into prostitution. When the father was interviewed at the sentencing hearing, rather than show remorse he made excuses and said this was nothing more than a case of entrapment because his son was a Muslim, and that his family was deeply hurt, humiliated, devastated, and embarrassed by the whole thing (his world revolved around himself). The article also said the father was just getting out of prison. I am sure that in the father's mind, this was all the result of bad luck... mostly entrapment bad luck. Seeing a pattern here? The father also stated emphatically that his son and nephew were not raised this way. Do you believe that? I don't.

Take a look at Ephesians 6:4, "*Fathers, do not provoke your children to anger by the way you treat them. Rather, bring them up with discipline and instruction that comes from the Lord.*"

The cycle can be broken. My mom was raised in a house with two pathetic alcoholic parents and was filled with terrible forms of abuse. She told me how thankful she was to break that pattern and raise three good kids. She fought her demons, of which there were *many*, by relying on God and refusing to be a victim. Two of the three children became doctors: one a PhD, one a medical doctor. We all married amazing spouses. I'm not naive; I witnessed her struggles while growing up. I understand it will be a harder journey for people like her, but it's still possible to break this horrible cycle with God's help. The good news is everyone has a loving Father who seeks and submits to Him. Parents, if your kids are in a bad environment, be a hero and get them out. Parents, if *you are* the *bad environment*, then *change. Fight for them, if not for yourself.* If you lose the first couple of rounds, keep going until you have won. It might not be easy, but I know you can do it if you want to. Put them in the best position to win, that is your obligation. Proverbs 24:16 says, "*For a just man falleth seven times, and riseth up again: but the wicked shall fall into mischief.*" What makes the person in this verse just is not that he falls down, it's that for every time he falls down, he gets back up again.

I'm not picking on anyone in this chapter, but my purpose for telling you these stories is I want this to be a teaching moment by showing you how much of an *impact* parents can have on their children, for good or bad. Can you imagine if any one of the above parents would have instead decided to dedicate their lives to Christ and live by His ways during their teenage years, what a difference that would have made. Finding a worthy husband, loving their neighbor, understanding all people are made in God's image, raising their children together in a biblical way – and finding their purpose in life? I truly believe if they had, history would have been rewritten, but that is just my opinion. I *believe* in *every component* of the family, and the importance of being a member of a loving family. Besides God, that is my *next strongest belief.* Strong families will make for strong individuals, which together go on to make strong nations. *Lead* your family well.

All that being said, if you're in debt up to your eyeballs, your kids will most likely think that is okay, and therefore normal. If your children see how important it is for you to drive an expensive vehicle you can't afford, they will grow up thinking this is an acceptable lifestyle. Teach them how to earn money, save money, and to be smart with money. They need to see you make good financial and lifestyle choices. This will go a long way in their lives.

CHAPTER 6

"License and insurance please."

I was raised in a small farming town in northern Illinois with a population of around 1,000 people. It's not on most maps. In fact, it's so small it doesn't even have a stop light. You'll find one gas station, one restaurant, and a school. That's about it. Most of the people I grew up with were working class people who didn't have extra money at their disposal. My dad worked a normal job as a loss control representative for an insurance company, and for most of our childhood, my mother was a stay at home mom.

In my opinion, success is something that almost anyone in America can achieve. It doesn't matter where you come from – if you have common sense, a good work ethic, faith in Christ, and plan well by making good decisions, you can succeed in a mighty way.

My sister was in high school when she told my dad she wanted to be a psychologist. She told him this was not her first choice; she would rather be a psychiatrist so she could have the option of prescribing medication when needed. Knowing her capabilities, my dad asked her, "Why not be a psychiatrist?"

"Because, I can't go to medical school," she replied. In her mind, she never even considered the possibility.

"Why not?" he asked.

She didn't have an answer. It was at that moment she realized she could – and would become a doctor.

My sister worked hard. She studied while her friends spent all their times at parties, and then she worked eighty-hour weeks during years of training. Her time of hard work in those early years really paid off. She met her husband in medical school, and now lives a very comfortable life. In fact, their house might be slightly bigger than the town we grew up in.

In life it's important to have a good support system. Surround yourself with people who will push you towards success. This lesson is both for the supporter and the supported. Be in a position where you can be someone's support and surround yourself with supporters, people you trust and have your best interest in mind. Over time, you can usually tell which friends are there because they care for you. If your friends are losers, there is a good chance that will influence your behavior as well.

Here's a story from my job that will demonstrate the importance of good friends. While on patrol in my fully marked squad car, I watched a white panel van completely disregard the stop sign right in front of me. I estimated he was traveling over 40 miles an hour. When I pulled him over, I asked for his driver's license and proof of insurance. Instead, he handed me a big stack of papers he retrieved from his center console and told me the insurance card should be somewhere in that disheveled pile. Oddly enough, on the top of the papers was a big chunk of marijuana. This was almost 10 years ago when weed was actually illegal.

I kind of chuckled and said, "Man, look, you just handed me your weed. I was only asking for your insurance."

The guy gave me a blank look and said, "Huh?" Then he finally noticed the huge chunk of weed sitting directly on top of his jumbled stack of papers which, coincidentally, had everything but his insurance card. He tried brushing his weed off the stack of papers. A little too late for that.

I placed him under arrest. I knew this guy had a lot more going on with him than just having a little bit of weed. Taking weed off the street has never been my main goal as a police officer. I joined to take bad guys off the street, and sometimes this was a way to do that. Criminals get away with many crimes during their lifetime because they can be difficult to prove. Taking them in on petty offenses is a way to remind them we're still out there.

Seeing the weed also gave me a reason to search the vehicle. To make the stop even more interesting, the passenger was intoxicated. As I searched the vehicle, the two occupants stood outside, waiting. Out of the blue, the passenger asked for "permission to pee in his pants." It took me a second to process what he was asking. Usually, people ask if they can make a phone call, sit down on the curb, but never had I been asked that before tonight. As I started to respond, I noticed it was too late. He was not embarrassed or ashamed. For some reason he made it a point to let me know he felt a lot better. I remember getting in my squad car and thinking to myself, "Did that really just happen?" I later found out that this odd type of behavior would be my new norm.

If his buddy could stop at stop signs and pay attention to where he put his weed, he might not have been out of a pair of pants. Lesson learned, be careful who you keep in your corner.

Chapter 7

Invest in Yourself, Don't Feed on Trash

If you are making decent money but your net worth is near zero or less than zero (meaning you are broke), you need to evaluate your behaviors. In America, the land of opportunity, being broke is a lifestyle choice. What are you doing with your life that causes you to remain in debt and live paycheck to paycheck? Sitting on the couch watching reality TV? "Escaping" from reality won't produce any return on your investment. There is a time and a place for relaxing and watching TV. I've been guilty of this before, but I don't make it a habit. Now, if I do watch TV, it is typically something I can learn from like a true story movie, a faith-based film, or a documentary.

I no longer watch the news. It's filled with violence, politics, misery, corruption and lies. The mainstream media wants us living in the dark under a blanket of lies. It is very *interesting* to see events I have been a part of regurgitated by a journalist in a different "style" that better suits the media outlet's agenda.

My favorite is when journalists offer their "expert" advice on police work and write a whole article on their opinion and feelings, rather than on facts or the law. A famous political reporter who worked for one of the major networks in Chicago for over 30 years spoke to a room full of law enforcement personnel at a training class I attended recently. During a question and answer time afterwards, she was asked numerous questions in various forms regarding bias in the media and fake news.

She readily admitted that inaccurate and biased news was currently a big problem in the field. One of the officers followed up and asked how things should change and what is the solution? She said, "Don't watch it or support it, honestly."

Those were her words, not mine. Besides being biased or inaccurate, I don't need to see the end result of violence to know I don't like it. I dislike most politicians, instead what we need are statesmen; something that is in short supply these days. I'll never understand why citizens in states like Illinois keep voting admitted criminals into office. You reap what you sow, and Illinois is currently reaping a bitter harvest. I know someone will get murdered today; a child will be left alone in a car or house while mommy dearest is buying drugs, visiting a John, or doing whatever she does. There will always be a politician in front of the camera speaking on someone else's good or bad behavior and vowing to fix it, making the same promise year after year while doing nothing to fix the root of the problem.

Where I live, the weather will be cold until May and hot until September. One political party will be blaming the other political party for anything and everything. Most of the media only cares about clickbait, propaganda, biased politics, money and power/control. I used to watch the news frequently – but I came to learn it was a waste of time. Don't let someone else "tell" you how you see the world. Use your own eyes to see the world as it is by viewing it through the lens of scripture.

Here is a verse that helps me not only with local voting and their *platform*, but also to understand who civil servants should be.

Exodus 18:21 says, *"But select capable men [women] from all the people – men who fear God [honor His laws], trustworthy men who hate dishonest gain – and appoint them, as officials over thousands, hundreds, fifties and tens."*

A relatively simple concept, but one that is often neglected.

Instead of feeding on typically inaccurate or biased information, I prefer spending my time reading non-fiction and faith-based narratives.

If you haven't read the book, *We Were One*, by Patrick K. O'Donnell, you should. It is a great reminder of how good we have it, and how much people will voluntarily give for a cause they believe in. If it wasn't for the Marines portrayed in this book who fought and sacrificed so much, many other Marines and Soldiers (including myself) might not be here today. Mr. O'Donnell was there shoulder to shoulder with these Marines, and his accounts of the battle of Fallujah are totally accurate. The events described in the book took place three years before my unit deployed to the same area. We went to Fallujah once a week for seven months straight. Many classify the battles detailed in this book as the most intense urban fighting since Hue City in Vietnam. On one offensive, coalition Forces lost over 100 troops.

I remember one day in Fallujah; I was standing guard outside a meeting when I noticed a mortar round impact crater two feet away. It most likely occurred during the battle mentioned in the book. I could see the fragment and splash marks riddled on the wall all around me. I wondered about the story behind it. Things really become real when you see the aftermath of a battle firsthand. It compelled me to feel thankful and grateful for the efforts of the Marines and Soldiers who went before me.

This image shows a bullet-riddled building along route Michigan in the heart of Fallujah in 2008. Most, if not all, of the buildings in Fallujah showed signs of war.

This picture was taken from our Mine Resistant Armor Protectant (MRAP) in 2008 as our convoy traveled over the Route 10 bridge, what we called "Route Michigan," in Fallujah. In Arabic, Fallujah means the "city of mosques," and the name is appropriate as the city is home to over two hundred mosques. This beautiful river is the historic Euphrates River mentioned numerous times in the Bible. Most people believe the Euphrates flows into the birthplace of human civilization, the Garden of Eden. In Biblical times the Euphrates also led into the area of Ur, Iraq where Abraham was born. This image also shows the destruction from Operation Phantom Fury in 2004.

The buildings were burnt, riddled with bullet holes and crumbling. During our deployment in 2008 we drove through with ease. This was also true when we dismounted and conducted security patrols on foot. There were obvious differences from November 2004 to 2008. People and cars were everywhere, and we had no incidents. If you don't know the following names, I suggest you learn them: Michael Hanks, Bill Sodja, Nathan Woods, Steven Wade, Sean Stokes, Sergeant Conner. The men I just mentioned are heroes, sadly most of us don't know their stories. This won't change unless we develop discipline and healthy habits.

My other second favorite book is entitled, *Particles in the Air*, written by my sister, Jenna Podjasek, MD. It is a medical thriller that won't disappoint. She's a very talented writer, and I'm proud to have her as my sister. I highly recommend you purchase a copy and read it.

I am a big proponent of reading, which is good for the mind. General Colin Powell said, "readers are leaders." According to millionairefoundry.com, 88 percent of self-made millionaires read at least 30 minutes a day, typically focusing on self-education.

Millionairefoundry.com also noted that millionaires take good care of their health, with 76 percent exercising 4 days a week. If I don't exercise every day, I feel it. I have less stress after exercising and I always think clearer because of this healthy habit. It is self-explanatory and I don't think anyone is going to argue with me about the benefits of exercise. If you are not carving time out of your day for exercise, you need to start today and never quit.

I learned a great deal through watching faith-based and true story movies. What better way to shape your ideas and habits than by watching successful and resilient people who are strong in faith? Obviously, Jesus is who we should model our life after, but we can learn a great deal from strong, courageous people. One trait most successful people have in common is they love to learn. If what you are reading or watching is not causing you to grow, you may want to reevaluate your mental diet. You might be feasting on mental junk food. Luke 2:52 sums up the youth of Jesus. It tells us that He grew in wisdom [mentally], stature [physically] and in favor with God [spiritually] and man [socially]. If we badly neglect any of these areas, it will adversely affect our lives.

Proverbs 15:14 reminds us that, "*A wise person is hungry for knowledge, a fool feeds on trash.*"

CHAPTER 8

I stood surprised. Not by the action, but how quick and insane the movement was. I didn't even see it. It took me a moment to realize what happened. Chalk? Who knew... at least now I know.

Each week, I look forward to checking our church bulletin for a Focus on the Family insert. The articles keep me updated on the real news around the world, including subjects the mainstream media refuses to "share" with us. The bulletin also gives practical family advice. One bulletin which stood out and helped change my perspective on this life, was titled, *The Pursuit of Happiness* by Jim Daly,

AMERICA'S DECLARATION OF INDEPENDENCE SAYS IT PLAINLY: We all have the right to pursue happiness. But many people never find authentic happiness because they become trapped under three common lies: (1) Life should be easy and fair. Take a look at the world around you. The fact that life isn't easy and fair is an obvious truth we can observe. And yet we get disappointed and angry when things don't go our way. (2) We should be better than we are. We struggle with our limitations. We think, what's wrong with me? I should be better than this. Many of us believe we should have no weaknesses or failures. But you'll never be happy if you believe you should be perfect. (3) We deserve more than we have. We think we deserve a better job, a better home or a better...anything and everything. If we can't be grateful for what we have and constantly think that we deserve more, then we're never going to be happy. Ultimately, more is never enough. If those three statements about creating happiness are lies, then their opposites are true. Learn to accept that life isn't fair and easy. Work to improve yourself, but accept that you'll never be perfect. Learn to be grateful for what you already have.

From a young age, my parents taught me life isn't fair. There will be times when you are wronged or mistreated, and there will be nothing you can do about it. While growing up, there were times it was difficult to accept that reality, but I'm glad they warned me. This knowledge helped me in the long run.

The truth of this lesson became all too real during boot camp. I remember the day well. Our platoon was getting ready for battalion inspections. Among other things, we were tasked with squaring away our greens, or class A uniforms.

From the beginning of boot camp, we were taught the importance of being squared away – often. A single mistake during inspection could mean failure for the entire platoon. Failure is not acceptable to a Marine recruit, and most especially, a drill instructor. Drill instructors are some of the sharpest Marines the Corps has to offer. They DO NOT like to fail.

In boot camp the recruits do everything together and at the same time. On this particular day, our drill instructor ordered us to work on our belts, which entailed cutting and placing our buckle at a precise length. During the time allotted to work on our belts, I was separately assigned to help our scribe with some paperwork. I wasn't allowed to work on my belt like the other 48 recruits. After a few minutes of working, the drill instructor on duty was replaced by another one. Immediately upon arrival, this new drill instructor bellowed for us all to get "on line" with our web belts (meaning we all stood at attention in front of our foot lockers). My heart sank as I realized he was going to check our progress on the belts. As we scrambled to get on line he counted down to from 10 to 1, just like every command is counted down and timed in boot camp. This drill instructor didn't know I had been ordered to help the scribe and wasn't ready for belt inspection.

The inspection was like the scene in Full Metal Jacket, where Gunnery Sergeant Hartman goes down the line inspecting the hygiene, fingernails, and blisters of the recruits. It was a slow and painful inspection because I knew what was coming. Keep in mind, boot camp isn't like school where you can raise your hand and ask the teacher a question. There are no excuses in this particular world, you either have your belt correct or you don't – period. In boot camp, you only speak when spoken to. You say, "Yes, Sir. No, Sir. Aye, Aye, Sir," all at the top of your lungs. Slowly, the instructor went down the line, telling each recruit what was wrong with his or her belt. "Quarter inch off, tenth of an inch off. Don't you $*&# with me, fix it now!' He had a huge block of chalk in his hand to mark the correct length, and I'm not talking about the short, skinny chalk teachers use. He became increasingly angry as he made his way down the line. I could feel my heartbeat increase and my quick, shallow breaths became louder as he slowly made his way to me.

I'll never forget his eyes as he slowly looked up from my poor excuse of a belt. It hadn't been measured and was likely off by inches.

His face and eyes said it all. The anger came at me like an explosion. It may have been a bad dream (if you've experienced recruit training, you've likely heard that saying before). The instructor "may or may not" have hammer-fisted my face multiple times with the world's biggest block of chalk. Was life fair at that point? Not really. Did I make excuses about it? No. I kept my mouth shut and took it. Did I mention all this happened four days before graduation? This was a time in training that was supposed to be a little less intense. Not for us. It was another lesson learned for me – never be complacent.

Even when the end is in sight, never let up until it's done. Besides that, everything is done for a reason in boot camp. I channeled that where it needed to be channeled. Let's not get confused. The United States Marine Corps is the world's finest fighting force. The USMC is not the Boy Scouts and it's certainly not summer camp. I learned that from my drill instructors, and I truly appreciate their commitment and service to us and the Corps.

In Focus on the Family, Jim Daly uses the word "deserves." In my line of work, I see a lot of people who believe they are "entitled" to whatever they want. This single word "entitlement" has such a negative effect on people. I can't begin to explain it. If you have a strong sense of entitlement and aren't willing to earn and contribute to society, I promise your life will never be rewarding or fulfilling. Please, don't raise your children with this philosophy. They won't be successful, or at least as successful as they could/should be. We shouldn't feel entitled to anything – ever.

Like Jim Daly said, life is not easy or fair. We think we should be better than we are, and we feel we deserve more than we have.

This applies in the area of finances as well. The furnace will go out when we already had an expensive week (not easy or fair). We feel we need to try and keep up with the Joneses. If they can afford it, we can too (in all reality they might be able to afford it, but you can't). Lastly, we don't deserve as much as we might think. We definitely don't need as much as we think we do. Your family deserves a roof over their head, food on the table, clothes on their back, to be loved unconditionally, to be taught life skills, the love of Christ, and that's it. It's that simple, that's what people deserve.

CHAPTER 9

A NOBLE WIFE

"A wife of noble character . . . is worth far more than rubies . . . She selects wool and flax and works with eager hands. She gets up while it is still dark: she provides food for her family and portions for her servant girls [whom she is teaching a good work ethic and skills that enable them to earn money] *¹⁶She considers a field and buys it; out of her earnings she plants a vineyard* [in some countries women are repressed in the market place and their economies suffer for it] . . . *¹⁸She sees that her trading is profitable* [honest profits are not bad, they are good]... *²⁰She opens her arms to the poor and extends her hands to the needy* [she does this out of love and generosity, not because of government compulsion]. *²¹When it snows, she has no fear for her household; for all of them are clothed in scarlet. ²²She makes coverings for her bed; she is clothed in fine linen and purple* [she is enjoying the fruits of her labor – as well as being generous to others. Those are not mutually exclusive activities]. *²³Her husband is respected at the city gate, where he takes his seat among the elders of the land* [he is involved in civil government, helping to maintain justice, without pay]. *²⁴She makes linen garments and sells them, and supplies the merchants with sashes* [she is involved in trading with people outside her own borders, which stimulates those economies as well]. *²⁵She is clothed with strength and dignity; she can laugh at the days to come* [through hard work and loving relationships with her children and family, she doesn't fear poverty in her old age]. *²⁶She speaks with wisdom* [which always begins with the fear of God and a deep respect for His laws] *and faithful instruction is on her tongue* [she is willing to bless others with the truths she has learned to lived by] *²⁷She watches over the affairs of her household and does not eat the bread of idleness.³¹ Give her the reward she has earned* [which means civil government needs to keep its fingers off of her wealth and not redistribute it to others]. (Proverbs 31:10-31)

The writing in parentheses comes from the book *Poverty of Nations* and my pastor, Mark. I agree with it. A noble wife is not a servant for her husband. I am sure that's what certain people are thinking, especially if you only read the beginning of the passage. The particular noble wife in this passage is actually the complete opposite of a servant. She runs a business, hires employees, teaches, and is generous to the poor. She glorifies God, is strong, relies on wisdom, and makes smart decisions. She is prepared, skilled, intelligent, and generous. She is loved and she loves. Her husband is respected at the city gate because she found a worthy man made from the same mold. She didn't marry a loser. She didn't look for her husband at a bar or the discharge area of a prison. No, she looked for him at her church, her place of employment, or took the suggestion of a trusted friend or family member. A noble wife is a great leader.

I can't begin to tell you how much my wife has taught me. She is intelligent, wise, compassionate, fears God, thinks things over, is detailed, and plans ahead far more than I do. If it wasn't for her I would be all over the place, heading in many directions at once. She leads by example. She lays her plans out and uses "to do lists." She has goals and enjoys accomplishments. She does not procrastinate, which is something I've always struggled with. She is good with money (I am sure you guessed that is important to me). She is generous to others and willing to help those in need. She's a great friend, a great mother, and a noble wife. She is a blessing and someone I wanted for a long time.

I remember a time when I was fourteen years old and dealing with a break-up. I was feeling a little down, so I talked with my sister about it. I told her I wanted to find a sweet church-going girl. This was how I saw it back then, but now I know that I was trying to say I wanted a noble girl. Thankfully, I got one, which was a blessing from God – that I didn't deserve. I fell short of God's glory thousands of times.

After we got married, I told my wife about that conversation with my sister. She found it interesting then told me of a time when she was thinking about what her future husband might be up to. She wondered if he was serving in the military in Iraq. It just so happened I actually was in Iraq at the time. I met her about a year later and the rest is history. We are truly happy together and each of us picked correctly. It helps when you are made from the same mold and have the same beliefs.

I am lucky to have met and married my wife. We fell in love, that is true. Even so, it is also fitting to advise others to cautiously pick the right person. Look at how she treats others, including her parents and other close family members because eventually she will treat you the same way. Find out what makes her tick. This is pretty obvious, but you *really* need to get to know her. Learn to dissect her characteristics. If your observations lead you to classify your significant other as: selfish, self-centered, cocky, narcissistic, or cheap, you might want to watch out. If you find she is caring, pleasant, happy, faithful, genuine, generous, treats others well, honors her mother and father, and is honest and grateful, you might be onto something. Try to find out how she treats those who do not give her anything in return. Does she inquire about you, or only talk about herself? Does she believe in something greater than herself? I think you see where I am going here.

Your date might be attractive, wealthy, have a solid career, and all those things are awesome. But if they are also narcissistic, cheap, shallow, rude, or treat others with disrespect, it will only be a matter of time before you start getting the same treatment. Do you want your children to be molded and guided by these negative principles? *Put yourself* in a *position* to find a *noble wife*. They say a married man lives longer than someone who is single. I would guess that his life will be even longer and more fulfilled if he is married to a noble wife.

If you are seeking a noble wife, be sure you can honestly be described as a worthy husband. On our second date my wife asked me if I played video games. Luckily I didn't, because she later told me that if I said yes, that might have been a deal breaker. She thought this would be an indication of what type of man I was, and I don't blame her. She was looking to marry a man, not a boy. Don't get me wrong, you can play video games and be noble and worthy. You truly can. The Biblical view of a husband is that he is a provider, a protector, and a leader – especially in serving his family. You can do all of those things and still occasionally play video games, but it will become a stumbling block if you play them several hours a day. Hopefully, that is self-explanatory.

My wife is thankful I provide for (she does too) and protect our family. We are both blessed and thankful for my job. I constantly remind her that being a stay at home mom is the hardest job in the world, and something that I couldn't do. Truly. With that being said, being "noble" means nothing if there is not a witness or someone on the receiving end. Don't be blind or indifferent. Tell her how much you appreciate her. Show her you appreciate her hard work and make sure it goes both ways.

A few years ago, I was at a point where I needed a little extra nudge in my Christian walk. I really wanted to learn more about the Bible but I couldn't get myself to open it. I was a believer but not quite where I wanted to be in my walk with God. She heard me complaining and making excuses about not understanding the Bible I had (even though I hadn't tried reading or understanding it yet). She bought me an NLT study Bible for Christmas, and reading it changed my life completely. Turns out the Bible wasn't hard to understand like I falsely claimed. I was a new person from that moment on. I submitted, repented, and asked to be used by God. Words can't explain how thankful I am for that little extra nudge my wife gave me.

Don't get this confused with perfection. She's not perfect, and I'm not perfect. I think it's pretty clear that no one who walks this earth is perfect, *not even close.* Jesus was the only one to walk this earth with perfection. I don't want to discourage you from finding someone without *all* these qualities, but you never will. Remember, people can change if they want to. This advice is not just for the person looking for a wife or husband. This is also for someone who might need to do a little gut checking (to be clear, I am talking to the selfish, narcissistic, disrespectful person who might be reading this). If they (or you) do not *want* to change, they most likely won't.

It doesn't hurt to have another set of eyes on the subject either, like a trusted friend, family member, or even a stranger who speaks the truth. Before we were married, I met my wife for lunch while I was on duty. She was always early and sometimes ordered the food before I got there so we could spend more time together. I only had a limited amount of time for my lunch break, and even that could be cut short to help on an emergency call. Whenever I got there, I always saw her seated at a table waiting for me to enter. When she saw me enter, she smiled with her beautiful smile and genuine eyes. I don't remember if it was right away or when we were leaving, but I heard an elderly gentleman say, "Excuse me officer." He proceeded to tell me something along these lines, "Officer, you got a keeper here. This pretty lady has been sitting and watching the door waiting for you to come visit her. When you entered, she was glowing and smiling ear to ear. You made her day, hang on to her." I always knew she loved me, but it was nice to hear someone else say it. I never have to worry about her not loving me, which is a nice feeling. Luckily, I didn't mess things up.

Let's look at Ephesians 5:25-28. "*For husbands, this means love your wives, just as Christ loved the church. He gave up his life for her...* [28] *In the same way, husbands ought to love their wives as they love their own body. For a man who loves his wife actually shows love for himself.*"

These verses come from the Apostle Paul, who was speaking about a Spirit-guided relationship between husbands and wives. My New Living Testament Study Bible explains these verses well.

Ephesians 5:25-30 – How should a man love his wife? (1) He should be willing to sacrifice everything for her (2) make her well-being of primary importance and (3) care for her as he cares for his own body.

Take care of your wife. Pump her gas at the gas station, hold the door for her, take her birthday off (your children's as well), tell her she looks beautiful, take her on date nights, thank her, support her decisions, encourage her, provide for her, and love her as you love yourself. I don't want my noble wife to take out the garbage, mow the lawn, or clean up our kid's stomach bug hazmat. My goal is to show her appreciation for being a noble wife by doing these unwanted tasks so she doesn't have to.

One last thing to consider, remember you are a team and should be able to motivate and coach each other. Make sure you are both involved and invested in the finances. Bounce ideas off each other and make decisions together. Be a noble and worthy team.

CHAPTER 10

HOUSING MARKET

A house is a big expense, and just like any expense it can be beneficial or detrimental. For most of us, our house is likely the biggest expense we'll ever have.

I recommend finding a well-built quality home. Keep in mind: just because it looks nice doesn't mean it's built well. If you discover the builder is now bankrupt, this should raise some red flags. Don't be in a rush and take time to do your research. For instance, did the company cut corners to quickly finish it? Is the company that built the house still in business? If not, find out why. Was the house built during a recession?

There is a neighborhood in my town that was built leading into the Great Recession of 2008. To mitigate their losses, they cut a lot of corners to quickly finish each house. I would never consider buying a house in that neighborhood.

There is a price for quality, but if it's true quality, it's worth it. Quality saves money and heartache. Before buying a home, ask a reputable and experienced home inspector who works the area you are looking in. Get referrals from people you know – like fellow church members or coworkers. My mechanic goes to our church, and one thing I never have to worry about is getting ripped off. I'm not saying all people who go to church are perfect or completely honest, but I would venture to say that your chances of finding an honest person in church is much higher than average.

Bring someone you trust who has a construction or remodeling background to your viewings. While thinking of where you're going to hang your favorite painting, or what color you plan to paint the wall, your experienced backup can pay attention to things you might not notice. Water damage stains, foundation issues, construction quality, moisture on windows, or mold issues are just some of things you need to be aware of.

It's ideal to buy low and sell high. Buy at wholesale and sell at retail prices. I understand that can be hard to do sometimes, but you should be paying attention to local and regional markets. Get to know a real estate agent you can trust. Be patient and do not panic if your house goes down in value – which happened in 2008-2011. If you don't sell it during those years, you don't lose any money. It will likely eventually go back up in value.

Some markets are overvalued while others are undervalued. If you are living in an overvalued area and sell at the right time, you can make a nice profit. While working as a bellman in college in 2003 or 2004, I transported a gentleman who worked for an online college to the airport. Everything was online, so he had the freedom to live anywhere. He stated he was from San Diego but recently moved. He timed the San Diego housing market perfectly. He bought his house for around $180,000 and was later able to sell it for around $750,000 and moved to the Miami area. With his profits, he was able to buy a house in Florida and a vacation house in the Bahamas.

Pastor Mark and his family also had the good fortune to sell in an overvalued market. When they moved from San Diego in 2002, they sold their previous home for over $200,000 above their original purchase price in 1990. Unbelievably, if they had waited three or four more years, they would have made over $400,000 on the sale.

Buy low, Sell high.

CHAPTER 11

MORTGAGE

"Owe nothing to anyone - except for your obligation to love one another."
(Romans 13:8a)

I bought my first home in 2010 on a short sale. This was after the housing market crashed but before it had time to recover. It sold for $394,500 (high) in 2004, $375,000 (high) in 2007 and to me for $256,500 (low) in 2010. Buy low, sell high.

In 2012, I married my beautiful wife. Our shared goal was paying off our mortgage – This was not a burden, we actually had fun doing it. From the time I received my first mortgage statement, I wanted to pay off my house. I knew the market would eventually bounce back, and if I was able to pay down the principal, I would eventually have some serious equity. I remember intently studying the mortgage statement. Then I crunched some numbers and realized if I made all the payments on time, I would end up paying nearly double my mortgage amount in interest through the course of the loan.

I heard people say things like, "The interest mirrors the inflation," and, "if you think about it, it's not really that bad of a deal." I didn't see it that way. I saw the whole thing as a gigantic rip off. I felt I was being taken advantage of. Let me be clear, in reality, I wasn't being taken advantage of; it was fair. I received a low interest rate, and I obviously agreed to it. I was not a victim – but it still didn't feel right to me ("Victim" will be a curse word in my house, along with "I can't." My mother never used the victim card, even though she very easily could have, and rightfully so). I also noticed the entire amount of the first payments went directly to debt. I'll be honest, I didn't know anything about finances at this point in my life. I learned as I went along, but one thing I realized pretty quickly was debt is bad. I didn't like it. I decided to do what I could to erase that debt and actually own my house. In early 2019, at the age of 35, we made the last payment. We paid our house off in eight years and eleven months. We now use the extra money to triple the money going into our investments. Coincidentally, we made a 31% return in our S&P 500 index fund in 2019. We made slightly smaller returns in our professionally managed 457(b) plan account. That is how you build sustainable wealth.

If you don't agree with paying your house off – that's okay – you are free to make your own choices. We can agree to disagree. However, if you've decided to pay your house off and need some advice, here it is. I strongly suggest getting a 15-year mortgage. If you can't afford the 15-year mortgage payments, you can't afford the house. Be sure you aren't spending more than 30% of your take home pay on your mortgage. Don't be house poor. That's a huge mistake many people make, and it devastated many financially when the housing market crashed (temporarily) in 2008.

Being I chose a quality-built home, it had the biggest margin to bounce back in value. I was lucky this was my first home; I didn't have to worry about selling another one when I bought it. I put

$35,000 as a down payment, even though my VA home loan didn't require one.

I kept another $35,000 in my bank to ensure I had back-up savings. I knew this would give me some wiggle room to make payments in the event we experienced a disaster or disability. After a few mortgage payments of paying extra towards the principal, my mortgage was down to somewhere around $215,000. My next goal was to get it under $200,000. To accomplish this, I downsized my vehicle to start getting the ball rolling in the right direction. One small victory.

After this victory, I paid as much as I could on the principal. At this time, I didn't use a budget, which I now regret. Instead of a budget, I made sure to always have at least $25,000 in my bank account. If my bank account was at $29,000, I paid my normal mortgage payment of $2,400 (mortgage and taxes included) and then paid an extra $1,000 towards the principal for a total of $3,400. I enjoyed relentlessly *attacking* the principal. It was my enemy.

Every spring I looked forward to my tax return. Not to buy a new car or take an expensive trip, but so I could apply my entire return towards my principal. Some years I was able to pay nearly $10,000. I loved getting a bigger check back around tax time rather than taking it evenly throughout the year because this forced me to save it. By my estimate, my tax returns alone allowed me to pay off approximately $60,000 towards our mortgage principal.

I have since changed my stance on this method. It actually makes more financial sense to get your money back during the year on each paycheck, instead of a lump sum almost a year later. It's your money, and if you have debt it's beneficial to attack it early. Not only that, I am letting the government hold my money, interest free for a whole year. I guarantee you they are making interest on that money, so why shouldn't I instead? You can make the decision for yourself, but I want to be open and honest about what I did, even if I don't recommend it now.

I realized each time I paid $2,000 on the principal; my monthly interest went down approximately $6. This may not sound like a lot, but when my principal was around $125,000, I was only paying $300 a month in interest. The $200 of interest I was now saving from the original $500 a month could now go to the principal. The more the principal decreased, the greater my attack against it. Through our constant "bombardments," the principal was getting weaker; we were getting stronger. My loan was slowly but surely disappearing. It was an amazing feeling. When we finally broke the $100,000 mark, we had a great feeling of euphoria. At that point, we were starting to get a taste of what it would feel like to be financially free. We didn't let up. We continued with our plan and by the time we paid the house off, the value had increased by approximately $100,000. Again, that is how you build sustainable wealth. That is how you create financial freedom.

With freedom comes options. Police work is a young man's game. As I got older I learned that chasing sixteen to twenty-year olds isn't as easy as it used to be. The fences get higher, and for some unknown reason the bad guys get faster. I didn't want to be forced into a physically demanding and stressful job as I approached old age. I saw the end result when older coworkers appeared to run out of options. No thanks. Options take time, start now.

Paying off our house was a move that paid off and will continue to pay off for my financially free family for years to come.

CHAPTER 12

PROSPER

The New Living Translation Life Application Study Bible defines prosper as, "to achieve economic success; to become strong and flourish." The word prosper occurs frequently in this book, and for good reason. Let me reiterate a few points to alleviate any confusion. I think people should prosper, and I believe God wants people to experience His blessings (Deuteronomy 28:11-13).

I don't believe in the Prosperity Gospel which suggests that looking at peoples' health and wealth is a way to gauge the level of either obedience or sin in their lives, and that if one is not healthy or wealthy, there must be wickedness in his or her life. Job's companions thought that. Read Job 42:7-8 to see the harsh words God had for their prosperity gospel beliefs. Like God, I don't believe that. There are many atheists who are both filthy rich and live a long life. By contrast, many believers struggle with their health and finances (II Corinthians 11:24-27).

Allow me to explain using a vehicle analogy. Before you can manufacture a vehicle you need engineers to design every aspect of the vehicle: engine, brakes, transmission, exterior, interior, etc. These same engineers, who know the vehicle inside and out, assist in making the owner's manual. This manual shows the owner how to maintain and operate the vehicle they built. It tells you what type of oil to use, the type and recommended octane of fuel, how much transmission fluid is required, when to change the tires, and what to do if a warning light appears. If you read and understand the manual and then do what it recommends, you will probably have a comfortable relationship with your car and it will give you many years of faithful service with very few problems.

But if you decide to ignore what the manual says because you think you know better; you will eventually suffer the consequences. Sitting on the edge of your seat while you listen to the manager at the auto repair shop smile as he tells you how much your new engine will cost is *not* a pleasant feeling at all. Waiting for a tow on the side of the road because you didn't follow the maintenance schedule is *not* comfortable.

The same can be applied to humans. We have a Creator, and being the Engineer, He knows how we were created to live. In America, loving God and following His ways usually means we won't have to live paycheck to paycheck. However, millions of Christians have suffered persecution and hardships because they do love God and live according to His ways. It's the people they live amongst who don't.

Sometimes upright people in the Bible, such as Naomi and Ruth, experienced poverty through no fault of their own. I don't believe Christians are guaranteed prosperity all the time, but God does give us an owner's manual that shows us how to prosper. There are hundreds of verses dealing with financial issues, and they are not put in there just to be "filler" material. Everything the Bible speaks about is important. And to be clear, how we handle our finances is important to God because He created us and *sustains* us.

Let's take a look at some workforce related subjects and see how Bible verses can be applied.

Job satisfaction – Proverbs 13:4, *"A sluggard's appetite is never filled, but the desires of the diligent are fully satisfied."*

Preparing for a job interview – Joshua 1:9, *"Have I not commanded you? Do not be frightened, and do not be dismayed, for the Lord your God is with you wherever you go."*

Work ethic – Ecclesiastes 9:10, *"Whatever your hand finds to do, do it with all your might."*

Let me close with my interpretation of prosperity, (which is a blessing from God.) To me, prosperity has nothing to do with having a personal driver in a Rolls Royce drop me off in front of an upscale restaurant. There may be a time and place for that, and I'm happy for someone who can do it. In America, this often means the person in the back has worked hard and *achieved* abundant wealth. What I'm saying is, having a chauffeur-driven Rolls Royce isn't what motivates me to work hard and prosper. What excites me is being able to enjoy time with my family. Instead, taking my wife, children, and grandchildren on a trip to see God's creation, or man's handiwork is my motivation to work hard. Most importantly, prosperity drives me to be a *good steward* of the money God *entrusted* me with to *manage*.

Pastor Mark shared this with me. Prosperity isn't the goal, it's one of the side effects of living a God-pleasing life. Denzel Washington said while giving a speech to recent college graduates in a stern and clear command, "Put God first in everything that you do." Mr. Washington gives great advice and is a prosperous man, not just a great actor.

The prophet Haggai was sent by the Lord to deliver this message to Israelites many years ago, and it is a great reminder for us in the present times.

"Why are you living in luxurious houses while my house is in ruins? This is what the Lord of Heaven's Armies says: Look at what's happening to you! You have planted much but harvest little. You eat but are not satisfied. You drink but you are still thirsty. You put clothes on but cannot keep warm. Your wages disappear as though you were putting them in pockets filled with holes!" (Haggai 1:4-6)

God's temple on earth today is the Church, which is God's ordained instrument for blessing all the nations of the earth. Many local churches are floundering today because members are too busy building their paneled houses instead of first seeking God's kingdom and His righteousness (Matthew 6:31-33).

When one prospers the way God *taught* us by *putting* Him *first*, it often helps others to prosper as well. A rising tide lifts all boats.

CHAPTER 13

NET WORTH

I experienced my first taste of wealth during my deployment to Iraq. There wasn't much I needed, so I didn't spend much. A story is told of a wealthy man talking to a poor man who claimed he had more than the rich man did. When asked how that could be, the poor man said, "Because I've got all I need and want, and you don't." When I came back to America, I had roughly $35,000 more in my bank account than when I left, making my net worth around fifty thousand dollars. Not bad for a young single Marine. I liked this feeling. For me, this was a substantial amount of money. I didn't splurge or spend it, I built on it. It became my sturdy foundation.

The easiest way to find out your net worth is to subtract your assets from your liabilities. Assets are items that provide an economic benefit or worth – cash, retirement funds, homes, and property. Liabilities are items you agree to pay for later (also known as a loan). If your liabilities total more than your assets, simply put, you're broke. If you have a family and your net worth is zero, or even slightly above zero, you are playing with fire.

It took me a while to realize this, but people in nice big houses with shiny new cars can still be broke. You can make millions of dollars a year and be broke.

Breaking down my assets and liabilities helped my outlook tremendously. If you had to sell and cash in everything, how much would you have to your name? Everyone needs to know the answer to this question. If your health fails, you lose your job, have an accident, or experience a death in the family, you are just one small step from placing you and your loved ones in a gigantic hole. Some families never bounce back from these disasters. Just ask your local divorce attorney.

In my opinion, families are supposed to have strong parents living in the same house. When I'm forced to work a double shift (16 hours) my oldest son will give me the cold shoulder the next day. Thankfully, after a couple minutes of playing hard to get he comes over and hugs me, wanting to play. Each day when I leave for work, my kids hang onto me and try blocking the door. My wife and I explain to them I need to work so our family has food to eat, a house to live in, and toys to play with. My oldest responds by saying he doesn't want food or toys, he just wants Daddy to stay home.

If you have a salary of one hundred thousand a year but no net worth, you need to rethink your priorities. Take a look in the mirror. Reevaluate yourself and your behaviors. Your kids don't care if you drive a shiny new car that you can't afford. Quite frankly, neither does the person at the stop light. I recommend that leaders of the family subtract their assets from their liabilities. Do you have your family pointing in the right direction? If you don't, figure it out. It's your responsibility as a leader.

CHAPTER 14

A TO B

D on't be like Mike until you *are* like Mike financially. There wasn't a day Michael Jordan came to the golf course where I caddied as a teenager with the same vehicle. Let me tell you, they were awesome. I remember looking inside his custom Range Rover and thinking, "I want one." I wouldn't mind having his Ferrari or Lamborghini either. I was still a teenager and luckily for my family, I grew out of that.

This is a picture of Michael Jordan's custom golf ball that I have in my possession. His vehicles, golf cart, golf bag, clothes and even his golf ball were personalized for him.

Remember, Michael Jordan is a billionaire and can afford any car he wants. If you are not quite at Michael Jordan's finance level, then be smart. Let me explain how much money he has. The first time I caddied for him I was paid to do just one job. Mr. Jordan had just received a custom set of golf clubs and golf bag with the North Carolina Tar Heel logo in famous Tar Heel blue. He requested a caddie to carry his new Tar Heel Blue putter – by hand – to prevent the grips from rubbing against the bag. I doubt he cared about the cost of replacing the grip on the putter as much as it was about the feel of it. Mr. Jordan didn't want any distractions while putting. He knows what it takes to win, and his ultra-competitive drive doesn't stop when he leaves the basketball court. When you can hire someone to carry one single club from a custom-made set of clubs made specifically for you, for thirty six holes of golf, you can probably drive whatever car you want. The goal is to win with money, not pretend to win with money.

In 1893, Henry Ford and William Durant designed an early Model T gas-powered vehicle. The main purpose for this invention was transportation. You might say it was to get you from point A to point B. At this time in my life, I own a car to get to work and back. If I lived closer, I would have walked or ridden a bike.

When I got married, my car was a Chevy SS Blazer. This was a vehicle I *really* wanted. Even though it wasn't the most expensive car on the road, it still cost a lot of money for me. I bought it for a little over $25,000 and put $10,000 down. My monthly payments were around $300. To borrow this money, I noticed my interest was a dollar a day, thirty bucks a month. Nothing crazy, but these dollars add up.

A few years later, I inherited a Honda Accord. It was over twenty years old, rusty, had over 145,000 miles, no air conditioner, and I had to pull the driver-side window up. It was not pretty, but it propelled my family towards wealth and prosperity while fulfilling its primary function, transportation.

Most people would sell the Honda, but I decided to sell the Blazer instead. Despite all the things wrong with it, I knew the Honda was a decent car mechanically. It had been my mom's car for over ten years and was well taken care of.

In my opinion the Blazer wasn't built all that well. It's primary appeal to me was it was fast and fun to drive. The one time I took it out and let loose, all the wadding from my exhaust blew out, looking like fifteen feet of grey witch hair trailing behind my car. The speed and performance was its biggest appeal.

I now felt like a fool. On top of all that, it only got about fourteen miles to a gallon. During this time gas was around $3.50 a gallon. I was spending close to a hundred dollars a week on gas. In a typical month I spent more on gas than I did on the car payment. Luckily, my Honda got almost three times better gas mileage, and it was paid for.

The Blazer had to go, even though it only had fifty thousand miles when I sold it. I put approximately seventeen thousand miles on it and lost $7,000 from when I paid for it. I deserved the fast vehicle, right? No, I deserved to prosper with my family. I learned in life, especially the Marines, you are not entitled to anything. When I had the Blazer, I wasn't able to attack debt, prosper, build wealth, or enjoy peace of mind. I estimate I paid about $250 more a month in gas with the Blazer than with the Honda Accord.

I still get ads from the same dealership asking me to trade in my vehicle for an upgrade. They promise to give me a great trade-in value, which is typically thousands below what I could sell it for myself. If you sell a car you usually need another one, which means you lost money on the car you sold and spent money on the one you buy. You lose twice while the car dealership makes out like a bandit. In the two years I owned the Blazer, I paid approximately $7,200 in payments. Between that and the added cost of repairs and insane gas prices – I stopped enjoying the car.

My "new" Honda Accord was nine years older, had a hundred thousand more miles, was very rusty, and sported a couple of well-earned door dings. Having liability only car insurance was exponentially cheaper than the full coverage on the Blazer. In reality, everything was cheaper for the Honda. It was well worth seeing the odometer roll over to 200,000. I know I can't compete with all the royalty out there doing amazing things day in and day out, but it works for me. I haven't made a car payment since selling the Blazer. As a matter of fact, in my 20 years of driving, I have only had a car payment for two of those years.

I know someone who bought a used luxury car last year for $28,000, (sales tax estimated to be around $1,680.) After realizing he didn't like the gas mileage or paying for the premium gas he was required to use, he sold it for $21,000 less than a year later. In ten months, the vehicle depreciated $7,000. Because he didn't pay cash for the vehicle, he still had a monthly $480 car payment to make. That car cost him well over $1,000 a month to drive.

My father-in-law's dad bought him a brand new 1972 Toyota Corona Mark 2 back when he was a sophomore in College. The price for this new car back then was $2,400, which was less than a dependable used Chevy. He sold it in 1982 for $1,700 dollars. The first thing that stuck out to me was that his first car was a Toyota, and he is still driving Toyotas today. Suffice to say he is happy with them. The second thing is, almost ten years later he sold the car for only seven hundred dollars less than when it cost brand new. Could you imagine if he would have bought it used? Toyotas are known to hold their value. If you want to build wealth, find reliable brands that are cheap to maintain, have good gas mileage, and hold their value. Unfortunately, luxury cars don't fit any of those categories.

If you are thinking to yourself right now, "Well driving a nice car is a status thing for me man. How else can the person next to me at a stop light (who I will never see again) know I am cool? And that is really important to me!"

Is a car what makes you important? Is your self-esteem so shallow it is built on the make and model of your vehicle? Enjoying fellowship with God, knowing that I am created in His image, living debt free, and serving my family and others is far more important to me – and far more important to God.

According to Forbes, Experian Automotive, a unit of the well-known credit information service, dug into their database of more than 600 million vehicles in the United States and Canada for insights. They discovered that 61 percent of people who earn $250,000 or more are not buying luxury brands, they're buying Toyotas, Hondas and Fords.

While at work, I accompanied two of my friends and coworkers for a meeting at our police station lobby with a successful businessman who started two companies from the ground up. He recently built a track and field facility in the community. He told us he built it to give back to his community by providing opportunities for underprivileged kids. He discovered very few collegiate track and field programs have athletes trained in hammer throwing. Therefore, even a young person with average skill would be in a good position to receive a college scholarship. Winners want other people to win.

Before seeing his vehicle, we all put our two cents in as to what kind of car he drove. Both of my co-workers thought he owned something luxurious and expensive. I said, "I could be wrong, but wealthy people don't usually drive those kind of cars. I bet he drives either a Cadillac or a Buick." Moments later I gave them both a wink. He pulled up in a Buick Lacrosse.

The owner and architect of the golf course I caddied also drove a vehicle below his means. This man designed the first integrated computer system for Wall Street. I don't know his net worth, but it is believed to be in the billions. There isn't anything he can't afford, including his own personal jet. He drove a 1992 Chevy 2-Door Blazer and was still driving it in 2004, the last year I caddied there. It worked fine and got him from point A to B on his 2,000 acre property without any issues.

This same person allows his alma mater, Northern Illinois University, to use his illustrious golf course as their home track for the golf program. He also allows his course to be used for the Arnold Palmer Cup, Division 1 Collegiate National Championships, and the Solheim cup. He co-founded and supports an organization called The Kids Golf Foundation and allows the local Boy Scout Troop to camp out on his property. He also supports Giant Steps and plans on building a residential component of independent and supported living for people with Autism on his property. He allows blind Veterans from Edward Hines Jr. VA Hospital, a local Catholic High School Fishing team, and Bo Jackson's Give Me A Chance Program –opportunities to use his property for activities such as camping or fishing. He also donated 20 acres of his land, along with 2.8 million dollars to build St. Katharine Drexel Catholic Church.

Be rational and smart with your vehicle purchases and pay cash. This forces you to buy something you can afford. Vehicles depreciate and you never want to get a loan for anything that depreciates in value. I suggest buying used and allowing someone else to take the new car hit. Most wealthy people focus on assets that appreciate, shunning anything that depreciates. Wealth is a state of mind. When I downsized and sold my Blazer in 2012, my mindset changed drastically. I saw how important it was not to have a car payment. The moment I sold the Blazer my family was *instantly affected*. From 2012 to early 2019 we were able to pay off the remaining $212,000 balance on our home. We started investing the way we should, and I viewed money completely differently. I had matured, and I liked it.

One last piece of vehicle advice; take it or leave it. I see people own a vehicle for eight years and never having any major issues with it. One day they decide "it is just time" for a new one. No major issues with the eight-year-old car, they have it paid off, but "it's just time." You might hear, "Well, I will start running into repairs soon so I might as well spend that money on a new car."

Yes, I have had repairs on my used car. In five years, I would estimate I paid less than $1,000 in repairs on a vehicle that was made in 1998. Good cars last if you take care of them. In most states, if you purchase a vehicle for $25,000 you can expect to pay around $1,500 in taxes alone. If it's not broken, don't fix it. That worked for the billionaire owner of the golf course I previously mentioned, and it will work for you.

CHAPTER 15

STEWARDSHIP

Generosity is a win-win for everyone. God makes us feel happy when we are generous because it's good. When we are generous, we are exhibiting the same trait God shows towards us, for he owns the *"cattle on a thousand hills,"* and wants for nothing. We see the same word "good" in Genesis 1:3-4. *"God said 'Let there be light,' and there was light. And God saw the light was good.* "This is the first time in the Bible God used the term good. God continued to use this word when he created the plants and trees, stars, birds and sea creatures, animals, and humans. Obviously, everything God created was good.

We see it again in Genesis 1:31, *"Then God looked over all He made, and He saw that it was very good!"* This refers to the last of his creations; humans made in God's image.

Giving feels good, it truly does. There is nothing wrong with trying to feel good (all the more when the giving is anonymous), especially in God's eyes. I believe we are created that way. Being generous creates a mindset that prevents you from idolizing money or yourself. It's not your money, it's God's money, you're only managing it. The correct Biblical word for this is stewardship. Many find it hard to practice stewardship in this area because money can have such a powerful grip on one's life. Sometimes, it's hard to imagine how a piece of paper can have so much power. It weighs almost nothing and takes up such small physical space.

Giving and generosity make two of the greatest commandments complete. *"Love God with all your heart and love your neighbor."* I don't suggest giving to support laziness or unappreciative entitled people, that would be enabling. Give to the church, first and foremost. But also give or support to meet a genuine need. A widow who lost her only source of income, someone whose health has declined and can't work, veterans organizations, or Christian mentoring programs. Support a good small business owner who has given their blood, sweat and tears to their business. Buy a Bible for someone who might need one, leave a good tip, or go out of your way to hire a tradesmen who has recently been laid off. There is always a need out there. If we open our eyes, we will see it.

Being a good steward with your money can set a good example. Generosity is contagious. One day while on the job, I met my dad for lunch and told him about a residential burglary call I just handled. The victims came home to find their house broken into, ransacked, and a lot of valuables missing. One of the missing items was $200 a 10-year-old had saved up. When I told my dad this, he asked for the address. He sent an anonymous letter saying he spoke to a cop who told him what happened. Enclosed with the letter was $200. My dad did this without even batting an eye. The ironic thing is, he has a hard time spending $200 on himself.

Here is some advice from the best financial advisor (Jesus) this world has ever known: *"Don't store up treasures here on earth, where moths eat them and rust destroys them, and where thieves break in and steal... Wherever your treasure is, there the desires of your heart will also be... No one can serve two masters. For you will hate one and love the other; you will be devoted to one and despise the other. You cannot serve God and be enslaved to money"* (Matthew 6:19, 21, 24).

There you go. It can't get much clearer than that. Yes, this book shows you how to be responsible with money but it is not a health and wealth type of book. Hopefully, you have been able to discern that by now. Being good with money is good for your family, and God makes it very clear that he believes family is important. It not only allows us to prosper, which is good, it affords us the opportunity to give to others or meet a need. But most importantly, it allows us to glorify God. If you are reading this because you love money and want to know how to make more and more and more, this probably isn't the right book on finances for you.

We just read what Jesus told us about earthly treasures and how easily they can be taken away. Some not only hoard treasure and power, they also idolize themselves – a huge violation of God's first two commandments. Do you remember the images of Saddam Hussein when the American Soldiers found him hiding in his hidey-hole? This man of wealth and power was unceremoniously pulled from a rat hole, filthy and distressed. At one time, he had enormous power in the world. At the snap of a finger, he could make any desire a reality. Saddam ruled by fear, as all dictators do. He envisioned recreating ancient Babylon under his watch, thinking he was a modern-day Nebuchadnezzar. But just like every other false god and tin-pot dictator, he was eventually destroyed. Saddam not only lost his lifestyle, power, money, mansions, and gold; at the end, he ingloriously lost his life. If you could have interviewed Saddam and asked him if it was all worth it, I wonder what he would have said? In this life possessions are all temporary. We have all heard the saying, "you can't take it with you." I have, in my possession, a piece of marble from one of Saddam's ruined vacation homes in the Thar Thar area of Iraq. Saddam was well-known for building lavish houses of gold and marble. This was some of Saddam's earthly treasures which ended up destroyed and left in shambles.

On top of the piece of marble is the Eagle Globe and Anchor that I earned on graduation day of boot camp.

Here I was, a Lance Corporal in the Marines standing next to another man's earthly treasure, demolished and in disarray (In case you are not familiar with the Marine Corps rank structure, Lance Corporals are still used in place of forklifts and maids). At the time, I picked it up and took it home because it was a part of history, like a chunk of the Berlin Wall. However, as I matured and grew spiritually, I later found out it was just one evil man's earthly treasure.

You can try to evade death but eventually your time will come. Even if you don't believe in God or Jesus, when you die you will be forced to bow before Jesus. Unlike the many choices you had in your life – as a result of free will.

Philippians 2:9-11 makes this very clear, "*Therefore, God elevated him to the place of the highest honor and gave him the name above all other names, that at the name of Jesus every knee should bow, in heaven and on earth and under the earth, and every tongue declare that Jesus Christ is Lord, to the glory of God the Father.*"

Do you remember when Jonah tried to run from God instead of going to Nineveh (in modern day Iraq) as instructed? Jonah learned firsthand he couldn't elude God, no matter how hard he tried. Deuteronomy 8:18 says, "*Remember the Lord your God. He is the One who gives you power to be successful, in order to fulfill the covenant He confirmed to your ancestors with an oath.*"

The New Living Translation Bible can explain this verse far better than me: "In times of plenty, we often take credit for our prosperity and become proud that our own hard work and cleverness have made us rich. It is easy to get so busy collecting and managing wealth that we push God right out of our lives. But it is God who gives us everything we have, and it is God who asked us to manage it for him." Think of it this way, our accomplishments, promotions, awards, raises, and employment are all solely because of God's blessing. Once you understand and believe that your entire mindset will change.

Let me make one thing clear. I do believe Christians can, and should, prosper financially. I don't believe we should give all our money away. You can search though the entire Bible, but you won't find anything in there about taking a "vow of poverty." If you believe in such a thing, like someone once said, "you must have gotten that out of the Bible, because it's surely not in it."

There is nothing wrong with being wealthy, it is a good thing. I do not believe in the forced redistribution of wealth, the Bible makes it very clear that giving is to be voluntary. If you do not work, you do not eat (2 Thessalonians 3:10). Obviously, this does not encompass those with handicaps, illness or injuries, etc. The verse is talking about the person who refuses to work and *blames everyone except himself* for not having or holding a job.

I was taught at a young age that you get rewarded for your hard work. Someone once said when a lazy person accused someone with money of being lucky he replied, "You're right, and I've learned something amazing. I can't explain it but the harder I work, the luckier I get." My time in the Marines reinforced this. It is good to adopt the mindset that everything should be earned. However, God wants us to remain generous and be good stewards of the money He has entrusted to us. Remember, monetary giving is just a small portion of this Stewardship. Giving of your time is very important because it is your most precious possession. You can always make more money, but you can't make more time. You only have a finite amount, and it can never be replenished.

Being good with money is good for your family, which is also good stewardship. Do not blindly throw your money, time, and resources around in the name of being generous, that is foolish. When you are truly generous, there will be times when your generosity will be taken advantage of and not used the way you intended. That's a reality, even if you are discerning there are always those who are experts at playing you. When that happens, and you have tried to be wise by spending time asking God to help you know what to do, and you still end up being taken advantage of that isn't on you; it's on them. And rest assured, God will square all accounts in the end.

Pastor Mark told me about when he was a new Pastor at Seaside, near Monterey, California and living in the parsonage next door to the church. One day, while outside making preparations for a youth camp, a dignified-looking woman approached him and said she needed a place to stay. With tears in her eyes, she told Mark, "Nobody cares."

Mark explained she could stay in the Parsonage temporarily while he and his wife were at camp until the church could help find a housing solution for her. Since the two of them would be gone for a week and the woman would be living here unattended, he laid out some house rules. Mark explained she would need to leave her cats outside because he was allergic to cat dander. She of course agreed.

When they returned home from the retreat she was gone, but not before leaving them a few surprises. The house was full of cat dander, and there were a number of very expensive long-distance phone charges on their next phone bill. Lesson learned.

Ten years later and 410 miles away from Seaside, Mark was working as a pastor in Vista, California when he came across a local newspaper article with a picture of "Ms. Nobody Cares." Of course, there were tears in her eyes. The article chided the community for not caring about this woman and other less fortunate people. It was obvious the journalist took her sob story at face value instead of doing his due diligence to verify the veracity of her stories and struggles before writing the article. Hopefully, that very caring journalist got her some real help, a hand up instead of a handout.

When Pastor Mark was at this same church, they fed over a hundred poor people twice a week in their gymnasium. This program was implemented before he became the pastor. One morning, while heading for his office, he noticed a young woman waiting outside who wanted to speak with him. As he listened intently, she readily confessed to selling drugs to many of the people the church was feeding. She curtly informed him that the money those people saved from their free meals enabled them to sleep in the park all day long where they bought and sold their drugs and alcohol - to party at night. When God convicted her of her sin, she repented and informed her buyers she would no longer sell them drugs, (be careful if you get in the way of an addict). After they punched her to the ground, beat her repeatedly and kicked her around, they found someone else to sell them drugs.

When the elders learned what was going on, they decided to begin partnering with a faith-based organization that understood the difference between helping and enabling. *Anyone* looking for *help* was *welcome* to come to their gymnasium for food, but they had to agree to be drug tested. Once this policy was implemented, amazingly, the number of people showing up decreased immediately. Those who were drug tested and failed were *invited* to come to meetings designed to help overcome their addictions, but until they tested clean, they didn't get fed. Those who were clean received a meal and instructions on how to fill out job applications and taught how to do a successful job interview. After a few months, many homeless people were now working and getting off the streets. Pastor Mark noticed that some people were drug free and working, but they were not quite able to make it to the end of the month financially. The church *gladly* helped them as well.

I've had many conversations with Mark, and it is apparent that he could write a whole chapter, possibly an entire book, entitled *The Parsonage*. He has heard and seen just about everything you could possibly imagine. The moral of the story is: Try to get to know people and do your best to actually help them – instead of enabling them. Try to give people a hand up, not just a handout.

Pastor Mark summed it all up by saying, "May God guide and assist us as individuals, and as a nation, to practice biblical compassion to those in need. Good things will happen if we do, and things will get much worse if we don't."

"Giving is the most selfish thing you can do" – Denzel Washington

Don't default to hearing the word "money" when reading what Denzel Washington has to say about giving, although money can be an important part of it. Also give of your time, money, love, hope and resources. Many wealthy celebrities throw money at the poor, but rarely will you find them "in the field" genuinely mingling with the "commoners" as they view them.

"It is more blessed to give than to receive." (Acts 20:35)

Psalm 23 sums it all up. Read the entire Psalm that was written by a warrior king (especially you warriors out there). Pay attention to verse 5 where David says, *"My cup overflows with blessings."* Some versions say, *"My cup runneth over."* I like both translations. This verse allows me to step back and take a look at all those things I *have*, *instead* of focusing on what I don't have.

"Bring all the tithes into the storehouse so there will be enough food in my Temple (which is how the priests of Israel supported their families).

If you do,' says the Lord of the Heaven's Armies, "I will open the windows of heaven for you. I will pour out a blessing so great you won't have enough room to take it in! Try me! Put me to the test!" (Malachi 3:10)

CHAPTER 16

O ne battalion sent 3,500 Marines into the fight. When they returned from the field, only about 385 Marines were fit to fight.

If you are feeling down about being snubbed or think life is treating you unfairly, please watch the documentary, *The American Experience: The Battle for Chosin.* In boot camp we learned about this very important part of Marine Corps history. One particular Marine battle that stood out to me was the "Frozen Chosin," a battle that took place by the Chosin Reservoir during the Korean War between 27 November and 13 December 1950. Marines, Navy, and Soldiers not only fought a ferocious enemy, they also had to fight and survive the elements and lack of essential supplies. During this battle temperatures could dip as low as -22 degrees Fahrenheit (-30 degrees Celsius).

In the documentary, one of the Marines, Juan Balleza, said this about the enemy soldiers. "Up to this day, if I were to meet a Chinese Soldier who was there, I would hug him like a brother. He suffered the same thing I did."

A Marine named Martin Overholt describes the long plodding march by foot from fierce combat and enemy lines into Hagaru. "I heard a Marine, who was not in the front line yet, say 'Look at those bastards. Those magnificent bastards.' Someone sang the Marine

Corps Hymn. Someone handed me a canteen cup full of hot coffee and a box of graham crackers. I just sat down in the snow. It was probably the best meal I have ever had in my life. That night I slept in my sleeping bag on straw in a tent (he chuckled to himself) and it was like luxury."

To be honest, I couldn't finish the whole documentary. It broke my heart watching Marines so cold they huddled against any available jeep engine for the tiniest bit of warmth. They were forced to survive on little to no food or water. They experienced such severe sleep deprivation that soldiers were falling asleep while walking. When you would take your boots off, you left some of your toes behind inside. You could say these conditions were so horrendous that you wouldn't wish it on your worst enemy.

Later, I reflected on this film. I thought about how good I had it in a war zone where it was warm. I felt ashamed but grateful. I had air-conditioning, hot food, water, and Gatorade delivered to our door by the pallet, along with hot showers, bathrooms, and a satellite phone I could use to call home every day if I wanted. A Portable DVD player. A platoon fridge, and so many other things the Chosin Marines could only have dreamed of.

I try to be grateful for my blessings; although, just like everyone, I sometimes don't appreciate all that I have. Like everyone else, I can find myself griping over what I don't have, or wish I had. Take a look around you. You have plenty to be grateful for. Being grateful opens your heart and mind. Being grateful makes envy disappear. It allows us to be content and become passionate and purposeful. Maybe I really do have more than I need. Maybe I can afford to tithe, donate money or time, and give to one of the thousand needy charities who do wonders for people. Once you learn to become grateful for what you have, it doesn't take much to see that your cup truly is overflowing. When I was in Iraq, I didn't have much to my name. I had my uniforms, weapon, portable DVD player, rack, roof over my head, steady income, my brothers, my honor, faith, my health, and my family. Yet, compared to many others in the world, that is a plenteous bounty. You might not believe me, but this is a picture of luxury.

This shows a makeshift room with just a single sheet of plywood separating me and my roommate from about twelve other Marines. I would say my "space" was about 8 feet by 8 feet. For a war zone we had it good. I mean, really good. Electricity, air conditioners, fridge, chow hall, and showers. Early in the war, Soldiers and Marines were sleeping in Humvees and eating MREs day in and day out. They took showers with a bar of soap and a bucket of water. No showers or air conditioners. You don't need much to be happy.

There was an awesome gym on base with any type of workout machine you could ask for. While going to the gym, I had the honor to walk on the Camp Habbaniyah street named Dunham Drive, named after Marine Corporal Jason Dunham, who lost his life when he heroically placed his helmet and himself over an enemy grenade to save the life of at least two of his fellow Marines. Cpl. Dunham was the first Marine since the Vietnam war to be awarded the Congressional Medal of Honor. He was a special man and an outstanding Marine. This man's heroism is highlighted in Michael M. Phillips' book, *The Gift of Valor*.

My mother told me she had a coworker who was a soldier in the US Army during the early part of the war in Iraq. The soldier explained how, in her experience, water was hard to come by and some days they were forced to take IVs for hydration. In America we take simple things like water for granted.

If you can't enjoy the things you have, you will always find yourself wanting more. That is an empty feeling which can be avoided. Be grateful for what you have.

Chapter 17

"Winners encourage others to win. Losers want others to lose." Dave Ramsey

I will share a Marine Corps acronym we learned very early on in our training that describes desired leadership traits: JJ DID TIE BUCKLE

Understand these terms if you want to lead others. They work.

Justice

Judgement

Dependability

Initiative

Decisiveness

Tact

Integrity

Enthusiasm

Bearing

Unselfishness

Courage

Knowledge

Loyalty

Endurance

I was fortunate enough to have leaders who modeled these traits while guiding me during my time in the Marines.

Peers

I learned a lot from my peers during my time in the Marines. When I think of my platoon in Iraq, there wasn't one of my peers from whom I didn't learn something. Toughness, grit, flexibility, and the ability to go with the flow was something I witnessed from my peers. The biggest trait our platoon had as a whole was a willingness to do something we didn't want to do. I will admit we had it pretty good. Our leaders treated us well, and there wasn't much to complain about. But whenever we were assigned an undesirable task, we took it and made the best of it. I don't remember anyone whining or moaning. It made life easier and increased the team's strength.

Lead by example. Backbone of the Marine Corps. Family for life. Pay homage.

I learned a lot from our direct leaders, Corporals and Sergeants in my MAP (Mobile Assault Platoon.) Most of them were guys who led by example. The most important thing I noticed was how easily they bonded and became family members with their fellow Marines from previous deployments – even more than I could have imagined. They told stories of heroism and loss. I remember how they spoke of friends and fellow brothers like Sgt. Matthew Adams, Cpl. Nathaniel T. Hammond and Cpl. Peter J. Giannopoulos, who were among 15 hero Marines our battalion lost in 2004. I was told Cpl. Hammond was liked so much by his fellow brothers that the company commander didn't allow any missions for two days after he was killed in action. This decision showed the magnitude that one well-liked leader could have on an entire company. I was told Cpl. Giannopoulos was killed heroically trying to load a TOW missile while under fire. He could've had a junior Marine do it, but Cpl. Giannopoulos understood what it meant to lead and understood the magnitude of being "the backbone" of the Marine Corps. It was important for us junior Marines to know what they did and realize they would never ask us to do something they weren't willing to do themselves. These were the type of guys directly leading us.

The family bond I witnessed proved true fifteen years later when an evil person in our police jurisdiction killed five innocent people and shot another person at his place of employment. Five of our fellow police officers were also shot as they heroically responded to that threat and saved lives. One of those officers was Officer Gomez who is also a retired Master Sergeant in the Marines. During our battalion's deployment to Al Anbar Province Iraq, he served as a platoon Sergeant of a MAP and the Mortar platoon commander for Weapons Company. The doctors later told Officer Gomez that he came within thirty seconds and no more than two minutes from bleeding out. The hospital ran out of his type of blood as they tried to keep up with all he was losing. Numerous hero officers came to his aid that day.

This started with a heroic extraction under fire and a wild ride to the hospital in a squad car. In between was a turning point in the fight, when a police officer and motivated retired Marine and his rifle changed the momentum of the gunfight. The coward didn't mind shooting at people from a hidden position, but it turns out he didn't like getting shot at himself. They did an amazing job and exemplified the hard to encompass word – Courage.

After the threat was eliminated, five of us jumped in a squad car and went to check on Officer Gomez at the hospital. I don't remember who arrived first, us or his Marine brothers, but Ofc. Gomez's brothers from the Marines somehow made it there very quickly. As time went by, I was amazed to see the Marines steadily streaming into the waiting room. The next morning, I went to the hospital and found the waiting room completely overrun by Marines. It literally was a madhouse which spilled out into the hallway.

The first person I saw was one of our fellow police officers who served in our same battalion. He had been through this before. In 2004, while serving in Iraq he was blown up by a mortar round. He died twice during medevac to the hospital but thank God he revived. He understood the importance of teamwork, which saved his life. He credits Marine Lance Corporal Ritter for saving his life by placing a tourniquet on him before he got medevacked.

The next person I saw was the Colonel of our regiment. Although living out of state, Colonel Smith was not about to miss supporting Officer Gomez and his family under any circumstance, even if he were dying of cancer. Tragically, he succumbed to his second bout with cancer about a month later. Master Sergeant Gomez later informed me that Colonel Smith was another favorite leader of his. Colonel Smith cared for his Marines so much.

This same group of Marines rallies up every Memorial Day weekend. Marines from numerous states travel to celebrate and remember the Marines our Battalion lost.

Assume the risk. Professional

My platoon commander in Iraq was a career Marine grunt who fully understood leadership. We called him "Gunny," which was short for Gunnery Sergeant. He eventually retired at the rank of First Sergeant, or "Top." He never yelled, but he never hesitated to let you know when you messed up or failed to perform like you should have. His look said it all. He expected a lot and demanded attention to detail, which we gave. He was stern but fair. When he spotted something that might have been an Improvised Explosive Device (IED), he went to investigate by himself. He could have easily sent junior Marines out to check on it, but he didn't. He assumed the same risks, exemplifying his dedication to bringing us all home in the same condition we left. He took his responsibility seriously and was never sloppy. He was a professional.

Address them by their name. What a Warrior is not.

I learned a lot from our battalion Sergeant Major just from watching him. Sergeant Major Scheerer was always in a good mood but knew how to turn it on when we were on the mission and starting to enter an unknown situation. No better friend, no worse enemy of a Marine. He was an extremely hard worker. Ten times out of ten, whenever I walked by his office to conduct late night radio maintenance, I never failed to see him in his office. In the Marines you are taught the importance of staying motivated through leading by example.

He overheard me talking about having a hard time sending videos I made for toasts at my brother's and sister's weddings. My internet connection was so slow it took roughly fifteen minutes to check and reply to a single email. Sgt Major's office had much better internet, and he gladly took time out of his busy schedule to help me out. Whenever he saw me, or any Marine in the battalion, he always addressed us by our name, which made us feel important. One bit of advice for you leaders, address people by their names. Sergeant Major led roughly a thousand Marines, and I wouldn't be surprised if he knew all of them by name. He genuinely cared about us.

I rode over 10,000 miles with him in the back of a Mine Resistant Armor Protectant (MRAP). During that time, I asked him about his various duty stations and all the different countries he had seen during his many years in the Corps. As he told me all the places he had been the conversation inevitably led to talking about war, which he never glorified. Whenever he told me about combat he broke eye contact. He experienced conflicts in Panama, the Desert Storm Invasion, and two tours of duty in Operation Iraqi Freedom. He talked about the enemy, (mostly eluding to soldiers in a conventional military like in Panama and the Iraqi Army, not insurgents or terrorists) in a way that made me realize the "enemy" was another human being. It doesn't change the way Marines fight, but why we fight. I heard this early and often from our leaders in the Marines, "We are not savages, but warriors." There is a big difference.

On top of all his duties, Sgt. Major could be found in the gym at all different hours of the day – even after a long mission. He showed many a junior Marine who didn't have nearly his amount of workload that we still had to make time for PT (physical training). He wasn't a do as I say person, but do as I do.

Bullet Magnet and Silver Stars

The Weapons Company commander during our deployment was Major Robert Weiler. I didn't work closely with him, but his reputation and actions had a great influence on me. The first thing that caught my attention was a unique rule of his. In his previous deployments, two of his field radio operators were killed in action. In war, the enemy typically tries to attack the radio operator first because they have the important ability to communicate with the company or battalion operation centers, where they can call in for such awesome things like an artillery or air strike. Due to this, radio operators were given the nickname "bullet magnets."

It was rumored that Major Weiler told the next radio operator assigned to him that he wouldn't carry the radio because he would assume those duties himself. I knew the Marine assigned to be his radio operator. He was a tough, south side Irish, Chicago kid. Carrying a radio didn't seem to faze him, even though he didn't get the opportunity.

Major Robert Weiler didn't just talk the talk, he walked the walk. He was awarded the Silver Star, which is the United States Armed Forces third-highest personal decoration for valor in combat. He was mentioned numerous times in the book, *No True Glory*, written by Bing West, which portrays Capt. Weiler's leadership and exemplary decision-making.

According to the official website of the United States Marine Corps, Captain Weiler led a quick reaction force that came to the aid of fellow Marines who were cornered. On multiple occasions he led his men to counterattack while facing a barrage of bullets. "I'm wearing this medal because of the performance of the battalion," Captain Weiler said. His calm demeanor allowed him to maintain control on the battlefield because he trusted his NCO's (non-commissioned officers who are said to be the backbone of the Marine Corps).

If the NCO's trust their leader and vice versa, watch out enemy. This unit will be a well-oiled fighting machine.

"He never broke a sweat or flinched," said Navy Petty Officer 2nd class Michael Rakebrandt. During a three-hour firefight, Captain Weiler repeatedly exposed himself to enemy fire to direct the unit counterattack, personally leading squads as they assaulted enemy firing positions.

"You could see him by his vehicle giving directions while bullets were flying by his head," said Rakebrandt, Senior Corpsman for Weapons Company.

If that doesn't motivate troops, I don't know what will. Rakebrandt said he re-enlisted just so he could serve with officers like Captain Weiler.

Remember police Officer G, who ran to the aid of his fellow man to stop an active shooter by placing others above himself. This same Marine, Master Sergeant G. along with the other platoon commanders, met and debriefed with Major Weiler every night for our deployment to Iraq. Master Sergeant G. said this about Major Weiler, "He was the absolute best commissioned officer I had worked for. Major Weiler was a bad ass and he made sure all of his Marines were the best they could be. I would do anything for him. Not only did he take care of us, but he worked us hard."

When no one was looking

During our time in Iraq, our platoon was in charge of the security and movement of the battalion commander, Lt. Colonel C. Towards the end of our deployment he approached me while I was doing some radio gear maintenance. The two of us were alone. He was not going out of his way to show others he was a good leader; he spoke with me on his own accord. He asked if I knew the story of Joe DiMaggio and Mickey Mantle? I knew both were legendary New York Yankees, but I didn't know any specific stories about them.

He went on to explain how the great Joe DiMaggio had been the center fielder for the Yankees a number of years before 1951. He became an absolute legend and hero to Yankee fans during this time. DiMaggio was nearing the end of his career due to a nagging heel injury. 1951 was the same year Mickey Mantle was brought up to the Yankees organization. They played some games together, but DiMaggio stayed in center field while Mantle played right field.

When DiMaggio retired later that year, Mantle had already established himself as a very promising prospect. Mantle took over centerfield and went on to arguably have one of the best careers in the history of MLB. Col. C. was leading into a story within our platoon. About a month into our deployment my direct leader was a Corporal who taught me everything I knew about being a radio operator in the field. Unfortunately, he was injured and ended up being transferred stateside. He was a combat veteran and knew his radios inside and out.

Col. C. informed me that he and Gunny initially had some reservations about giving me the reins as the battalion commander, and platoon radio operator (each separate billets) as a Lance Corporal. Gunny didn't want to mess with the chemistry of the platoon, which is very important, by bringing an outsider into the platoon a month into our deployment. Gunny had already relieved one radio operator before our deployment, opening the spot up for me. The gamble paid off. Our platoon was a tight-knit group and we all got along. Following my taking over all communication responsibilities, there were no major communication incidents during the rest of the deployment.

The battalion commander didn't need to take time out of his day to tell me this story or thank me, but he did. It actually meant a lot to me because I didn't start off so hot earlier in the deployment. I worked hard trying to hold my end of the bargain up. He thanked me and gave me his challenge coin. I know he went out of his way to thank and praise a lot of other Marines in our platoon and battalion, and I'm sure they enjoyed his praise as well. I respected his honesty with me. Truth is very important in life, and you can learn a lot from someone who has enough of a backbone to tell you the raw unbridled truth. Being compared to a guy like Mickey Mantle was pretty cool. That is what leaders do.

Leaders care about others, and they motivate others to keep up the good work. My Gunny later put me in for a meritorious promotion to Corporal, (NCO) and A Navy and Marine Corps Achievement Medal. I was awarded both, which needed the Sgt Major and Battalion commander's approval. I was never really concerned about the actual award, but it meant a lot to receive a "head nod" from my leaders. This lit a fire, motivating me to be part of the next generation of Marine leaders. I always made sure to encourage and praise my Marines' good work while sometimes correcting them. I let them know I trusted in them and tried my best to set them on the right path towards success. I know my Marines would follow me into war, and they trusted in my path. My hope was when I retired, my Marines would be followed and trusted by their Marines as well – and so on.

If you want to see leadership exemplified firsthand watch the *Medal of Honor* series on Netflix. They did a great job portraying how truly special these men are. A couple common characteristics you will see with all the Medal of Honor recipients is selflessness and a love for their brothers.

Observations during my time in the workforce

Below is another set of leadership traits I observed during my experience in the workforce. I believe these traits are translatable into any job. If you understand and live by them, you will improve as a leader and add inestimable value to your team.

Humble

Genuine

Cares about the welfare of all people

Courageous

Moral

Makes intelligent decisions

Does not conform - has a backbone (in my opinion having a backbone is mandatory)

Rock steady

Resilient

Comfortable with self, knows who he/she is.

Knows their own strengths and weaknesses

Leads by good example

Knows how to communicate clearly, listens to the troops

Knows their troops and knows what makes them tick

Provides and encourages room for growth

From my experience the worst type of leaders are ones who have these traits:

Haughtiness

Unorganized

Contradictory

Know-it-all

Micro manager

Wavering

These are my experiences and views on leadership. But now let's ask an expert. Master Sergeant (USMC Retired)/Police Officer Gomez was gracious enough to write about his personal experiences and what he envisions leadership to be.

I'm not sure if I can summarize leadership into words, but I will give it a go. In over 20 years in the Marines, I learned a lot about leadership, the good and bad. I have had good leaders and not so good ones. I always learned from both and learned what to do and what NOT to do.

One of the most important things I learned was to "Always lead from the front." Yes, that is easy to say and harder to do. This requires dedication to lead, as well as integrity to do it. Integrity to do the right thing even when no one is watching. Leading from the front to me means never asking someone to do something you are not willing to do yourself or have done yourself. In combat this will go a long way. You never want to be that guy who says, "just do it because I said so," especially if your men know you are not willing to do the same as them.

Another valuable leadership rule I learned, and this goes a little rogue in Marine standards. Let me explain. In the Marines there are two leadership goals: Mission Accomplishment and Troop Welfare. Mission Accomplishment is thought to always come first. To a degree I concur with this, but I have learned if you're able to balance these two goals, Troop Welfare should always come first. I have learned that when you take care of your men, when you train them to be the best and the most proficient, and also treat them with the utmost respect, they will accomplish the mission every time. You have to take care of their needs, listen to their problems and fix them so that they will be able to dedicate their energy and mind to accomplishing the mission.

Both of these leadership lessons, I was able to see first-hand with two great leaders I worked for. Colonel Mark A. Smith and Lieutenant Colonel Robert Weiler. Colonel Smith was the Battalion Commander Officer during my first combat deployment, and I was his personnel security detachment (PSD) Platoon Sergeant. What I saw of Col. Smith was his honest and deep care of his Marines. I saw that man weep every time we lost a Marine, as if it were his own son.

Yet, he pushed on and continued to fight through the pain and accomplished the mission. At times it was hard to keep him safe, (which was PSD's mission) as he would dismount our trucks during patrols like he was a junior Marine tasked with security during a halt. He would be the first out of the truck and the last one in. If you are a young Marine and see a Battalion Commander out there risking his life during a patrol or security halt, then you will be motivated to do the same. Fifteen years after we returned home, I saw Col. Smith from time to time at reunions and memorial outings. He still wept for our fallen and cherished the time spent with his Marines. When I was shot during Henry Pratt, he reached out to my wife and simply said, "What hospital and where is the nearest hotel, I'm en route! "He was at my side and in the hospital every day until I was in the clear. After leaving the hospital, he checked in on me and my wife. What we did not know is that he would lose his fight with cancer just a few weeks after. The last thing I will remember of Col. Smith is that he stood by his injured Marines and took care of them until his last breath. Man, wouldn't you love to be led by men like that?

Another example of great leadership was Lieutenant Colonel Weiler. He was known as "The Wookie" because he was a giant man who could tear your arms off your body. At the time his rank was Major, and he was our Company Commander during our second deployment. Major Weiler was actually not required to deploy as our Company Commander. He was the active duty staff liaison for our reserve unit. Major Weiler was asked to deploy as the Battalion Executive Officer (XO) but refused. Major Weiler said he would deploy as the Weapons Company Commanding Officer. We had heard stories of Major Weiler in Ramadi and his being awarded a

Silver Cross for heroism. He was an intimidating man, but as we worked more and more with him, we learned he was a teddy bear (but never tell him I said that). During our work-up for our second combat deployment he worked harder than anyone I have ever served under. We trained all the time. We would spend 5 to 10 days out in the field at a time. We would train with every piece of equipment, every weapons system, and conduct patrols and drills until we were near perfect. You would think we would hate him for this. Not a damn chance. We absolutely loved him. After each field operation, he would give us 4-day weekends even when the higher ups disagreed. He would have beer and pizza waiting for us after every field operation, so we could enjoy a cold one and pizza while cleaning weapons and gear. This was not liked by higher ups, but he didn't care. If we gave him our all, he in return would do anything to take care of us. Major Weiler motivated us to be the best. In fact, our company of reservists was hands down the best in the Battalion, and I would put money that it was the best in Iraq. To back that, the Commanding General of forces in Iraq, General John Kelly, would visit our combat outpost and make the same comment about Weapons Company 2nd Battalion 24th Marine Regiment. It was all because of Lt. Col. Weiler's leadership.

I also want to talk about three friends of mine who died being leaders. Our first loss was not in battle, but during our work up for Iraq. Sgt. Matthew Adams was killed in a training accident in San Diego. During a mock patrol and driving exercise, Sgt. Adams was a vehicle commander for one of his platoon's HMMWV's. During the exercise he switched places with his gunner so he could feel more comfortable being in the turret during the driving exercise. Sgt.

Adams wanted to show his men that he would never ask them to do something he was not willing to do himself. During the exercise, the HMMWV flipped over and landed on Sgt. Adams, killing him instantly.

His death was devastating to not only us, but the entire battalion. Sgt. Adams was my roommate and close friend. His death set a precedent to all leaders in the unit. We would always lead from the front and show the junior Marines that we will never ask them to do anything we were not willing to do ourselves. We would be the first to the door and the last one out.

Our second loss for our company was Corporal Nathaniel Hammond. Cpl. Hammond was killed by an IED during a combat patrol near Yusufiyah, Iraq. During a security halt, the platoon was to dismount and check the area for IEDs. Cpl. Hammond was the first to exit his vehicle and conduct his 5s and 25s checks with the rest of his Marines. During his check of the area the enemy detonated an IED and Cpl. Hammond was killed instantly. He could have told his Marines to conduct the checks while safely remaining inside the safety of the armored vehicle. Instead, he led his Marines, and paid the ultimate price. He again showed that true leaders lead from the front.

The third loss of our deployment was Corporal Peter "Gino" Giannopoulos. Gino's platoon was ambushed near Latafiyah, Iraq. During the firefight they were met with heavy machine gun fire from a dug in position. His turret gunner was armed with a TOW missile. The heavy machine gun fire damaged the loaded missile right when the gunner was about to shoot it. Gino exited his armored vehicle, exposing himself to heavy enemy fire as he ran to the back of the vehicle to retrieve a second missile. While retrieving the missile, Gino was shot by the enemy. He was medically evacuated but succumbed to his wound during transport. This again showed that true leadership puts others before self.

What I learned in my 21 years of service in the Marines, and primarily from these two men, made me a better leader. These men taught me to care about those you lead, and in return they will do the same. I would do anything for these men. I would walk on fire if they asked me to because I know they would do the same for me. I would die trying to accomplish any mission they gave me because I know they would die trying to take care of me. Although it is hard to say, "Yes, I am a leader," I hope that I can be viewed as one. One day I hope to be a leader like those who taught me to be a better leader, a better man, a better husband, son, brother, father, and friend.

I first met then Gunnery Sergeant "Gunny" Gomez while in Iraq. I was on the hiring list for the same department he was currently working for. Gunny's leadership reinforced why I wanted to work in that department. I heard many good things about Gunny, and I still remember the first time I met him. Little did I know I would eventually work with him at the department with the same six-person squad for over seven years. I sat back, watched and learned. I looked up to him in 2008, and I look up to him even more today. We were involved in an officer involved shooting together, conducted numerous undercover surveillance details, and chased the same bad guys around town for almost 10 years after meeting each other. I would not ask just "anyone" to share their personal life and views. When I say legit, I mean legit. Take note.

***

My first partner in the community policing unit taught me one of the most important lessons I learned as a police officer – simply lead by example. This officer always had sticker badges in his vest to hand out to young kids. Whenever he saw a kid smile, wave, or even look our way he handed them a sticker badge. The kids loved it, and their faces lit up with joy. It was great for the parents to see. This was a great form of human connection. During a training class I attended the instructor told us a story about how his six-year old son literally believed police officers had superpowers. This was more than a sticker badge to the kids and their parents. I learned by watching to always have sticker badges on me.

A Chicago PD officer reached out to our unit to see if we could assist him and his team in apprehending a bad guy who might be hiding out in our town. The officer was part of a robbery task force specializing in solving and apprehending criminals who commit armed robberies. In this case the bad guy had been committing armed robberies in their jurisdiction but recently increased his level of violence when he killed a store clerk.

My partner and I stood by while their task force engaged in surveillance. Our job was to conduct a traffic stop if his vehicle left the apartment complex since we had a marked police car. On the second day, his vehicle finally ended up leaving and we conducted the traffic stop. I was the senior officer in the squad car. I didn't preach, but I was open with my faith. I don't have a problem telling people close to me that, "I know where I am going when I die." I don't say something unless I am prepared to back it up, and I use this as "proof" of my faith.

I told my partner that I would approach the driver, even though my partner was the driver for the day. Our practice was the driver approaches the driver of the vehicle while his partner watches everything else from the side/rear of the vehicle. I told him to stay back on the passenger side rear of the vehicle while I approached the bad guy. I did this so if the bad guy started throwing rounds our way, my partner would have a better chance of survival from his position. The two of us spent two years on the road together, and he was like a member of my family.

Both our adrenaline levels were elevated, as we could both picture this traffic stop getting interesting. We had a pretty good feeling that the bad guy knew the task force was looking for him, which meant he might be willing to do anything. Right or wrong, as far as I saw it, it was my responsibility as the senior officer and as a Christian to make contact, even though my partner most likely wanted to initiate contact to protect me. Things happen fast and there isn't always time to iron out the details. In our world, once a tactical decision is communicated, the other person reacts off that decision, no questions asked. There isn't time to discuss options or change game plans, that's it.

Unfortunately, it was the bad guy's nephew driving the car and not the murderer. I did make a friend though. Whenever I saw his nephew walk through the neighborhood he made sure to take time out of his busy day to wave at me with one finger. It always makes me smile, that's what good friends are for. Luckily, a month or so later, the task force picked up his uncle outside our jurisdiction without incident. Sometimes you will need to stick your neck out for others as a way to let your light shine. People will notice, and hopefully this will make them think. Saying things like, "I know where I am going when I die," and trying my best to live that way is my way of preaching to others around me.

I watched and learned from one of my field training officers who did something very similar. While in training as a new recruit, we stopped a car, knowing the driver was supposed to have a firearm in his possession. While I was trying to remember my name and where I was, my field training officer told me, "Stay back, I got this." That's what leaders do.

Leader or boss?

Which person do you think is better for your organization – a boss or a leader? Do you think the troops will work harder and be more efficient working for a boss or a leader?

In my opinion boss systems only work effectively if you have a bunch of yes men/women. I do not respect yes men/women, and I certainly do not want them on my team. I would take an average worker who cares about the team over a "hard worker" who doesn't. In what sense are they "hard working"? Yes men only value *their* accomplishments and promotional standing. I have been on sports teams since I was six years old. During that time, I have only been on losing teams twice, and I still remember that losing feeling. I played on approximately twenty winning teams since then; I know how a team should function at a winning level versus a bunch of individuals.

I talked about this in my stewardship chapter, but it also applies to leadership. While speaking with my dad, I told him about the incident where a ten-year-old and his family were victims of a residential burglary. The family lost a lot of expensive goods and the kid lost $200 from his savings. My dad mailed the ten-year-old victim two hundred dollars. This was of course anonymous (I guess not anymore). I have been fortunate to watch and learn from people with big hearts. That is the quintessential example of leading by example.

Hebrews 13:7 says "*Remember your leaders, who spoke the word of God to you. Consider the outcome of their way of life and imitate their faith.*"

***

It is okay to experience weakness and defeat at times. When it happens, try to learn from it and fix it. If you get knocked down, how do you respond? Do you get back up and what do you do about it? Proverbs 24:16 says, "*For a just man falleth seven times, and riseth up again: but the wicked shall fall into mischief.*" You will never be perfect – but remember, people are watching. Humble people make great leaders.

I won't forget the time we were at a Sheik meeting somewhere around the city of Ramadi, Iraq. Usually, a family member of the Sheik would offer us some food like kebabs, rice and chi tea. We were encouraged to eat it and not be rude. Besides, I really enjoyed the local food. We would rotate security duties to eat. This one particular day, a couple of us Lance Corporals were sent inside to grab some lunch. I think there were four of us and maybe four Iraqi police officers. They came over and asked us about our gear. "Mister, what is this? Mister, how America? Mister what is Marines?"

After some more questions and answers, one of the Iraqis asked if I would arm-wrestle his friend. I knew something was up. The guy was small and didn't appear muscular or strong. He had a dumb look on his face with a slight smile, but I had been lifting and working out every day for five months. I was in the best shape of my life, so if I was going to beat him, now was the time. I was hesitant but expected to win. This guy started to get in the zone when I sat down, stretching and moving his body into a professional looking arm wrestler's stance. We both sat down, arms locked while exchanging mean looks at each other.

Ready, set, go. It was over before it started and I didn't stand a chance. Okay, I was set up, and I lost. Big deal. It was a lesson in humility. Even though I am extremely competitive and hate losing, I had to swallow my pride.

At the time I did not understand humility. I never understood why Pastor Mark always mentioned humility as being a good thing. Why would I want to be humiliated? Where are they finding these pastors anyway? Luckily, I now know why it is so important. My guys still respected me, and I took it as a learning experience. Next time I get challenged to an arm-wrestling match in Ramadi, I will tell a *little* lie and claim my shoulder is recovering from a recent surgery. The lesson learned – looks can be deceiving, and strategy is very important. Luckily, we ended up leaving the lunch with a victory. One of the other Lance Corporals volunteered to go next – and beat him.

Professionals

Way back in the year 2000 or 2001, I caddied for a professional golfer. Mr. Steve Stricker was playing at the illustrious Rich Harvest Farms private golf club. I was just a teenager but Mr. Stricker made quite the impact on me. He was genuine, humble, and treated everyone fairly. I can confidently say he was genuine because he treated me like an equal, even when no one was looking. I will never forget that. This taught me a lot. He didn't need to treat a caddie well, especially when no one was looking, but he did. As a police officer I try to apply that lesson to everyone I meet on a daily basis, including homeless people, mentally unstable people, and even criminals.

One day, while warming up prior to a tournament, Mr. Stricker helped the best golfer in the world, Tiger Woods, with his putting even though they were competitors. Mr. Stricker finished runner-up to Tiger by two strokes in that same tournament. You might hear this again, but winners want other people to win and losers want other people to lose.

To date, Mr. Stricker has twelve PGA tour victories and five PGA Tour Champions victories. Mr. Stricker has been either the "captain" or "vice-captain" for the American Ryder Cup the last four events. I am proud to say that Mr. Steve Stricker was appointed as the prestigious 2020 Ryder Cup Captain of the American Team. This is the pinnacle for a leader in golf. It is very apparent why he was selected, and I'm sure everyone who meets or knows him feels the same way.

Mr. Stricker prioritizes family by not playing in every available tournament. He is the kind of guy you want on your side, a real class act. From what I have read, and based on my experience, he leads his family and anyone he comes in contact with – well.

Another professional golfing legend I caddied for was Dave Stockton. Mr. Stockton was also a genuine guy I learned a lot from. He wanted others to excel and proved it every time he gave other golfers advice on putting. He treated others like equals and talked to people about more than just golf. Mr. Stockton asked if I could caddie for him and his son, Dave Stockton Jr., the day after a tournament while they played a leisurely round of golf. He didn't change the way he treated me when it was just the three of us. That was the most fun I ever had as a caddie; watching those amazing golfers nonchalantly but perfectly strike the ball within feet of the pin.

Below Par Leaders

Keep this in mind. The reality of life is, you will inevitably run into bosses who are below par in your life and in the workforce. When you have these unfortunate encounters, don't let it get the best of you. Instead, consider it a learning experience. Remember, if nothing else a person can serve as an example of what not to do. You can learn just as much about leadership, maybe more, from watching below par leaders as you can by watching good leaders. There is a lot to be said about the person who is liked by his bosses but disliked by those under him. If you treat people above you differently than the way you treat those below you then you might be doing something wrong.

Treat all people well because you want to, not because you want something from them.

Philippians 2:3 says, "*Do nothing out of selfish ambition or vain conceit rather, in humility value others above yourselves, not looking to your own interests but each of you to the interests of the others.*"

Chow line lessons

I learned this tradition while serving in the Marines: Never eat before your troops. This applies to when you are in a setting where a whole company or platoon is being fed at the same time. The lowest rank goes to the front of the line and then on up to the NCOs. Make sure they are taken care of first, and if you are in a position of rank, you go last.

All-American boy, skinny quiet Marine and the Marksmanship Instructor

Anyone can be a leader and we need more good people to step up and lead. This next story demonstrates that the leader does not always have to be the biggest, strongest or best-looking person.

During boot camp our platoon was tested on numerous subjects and activities, including our performance on the rifle range, battalion drill, uniform inspections, physical fitness tests, field day, and swim qualifications. Naturally, being Marines, these tests turned into a competition amongst platoons. For some reason, on many of the tests our platoon ranked near the bottom. Luckily for us, our next training exercise was the rifle range.

Our platoon was assigned a Primary Marksmanship Instructor who was rumored to be the best instructor (which turned out to be true). True to Marine tradition, we snapped in and dry fired for a week while our PMI taught us everything we needed to know about marksmanship. He could tell that a couple of us had their heads low and lacked confidence. He sat the whole platoon down and told us a real-life story he witnessed about a "skinny quiet Marine" and the "300 PFTer".

A 300 PFT is a perfect score on the Marine Physical Fitness Test. This Marine was described as a muscular all-American boy. A lot of Marines in his platoon looked up to him because of this, not because of who he was. By contrast, the skinny Marine was not very popular and quiet. Want to be tested? Go experience combat. There is no faking leadership when you are playing for keeps. When the bullets start flying, you will see the real leaders step up and separate themselves from the rest of the group.

When their platoon got their first taste of what our PMI described as a "hot zone" (this means they were thrown into the fight and did not have much time to acclimate to war), the all-American boy froze up with shell shock but the skinny Marine was in his element and undaunted. When they had to attack a building full of insurgents, the skinny Marine showed why he was in his element.

He volunteered to be point man and entered a room occupied by an insurgent with a machine gun. They had already taken rounds from the insurgent and knew for a fact he was in there. When he heard the insurgent reloading, the skinny Marine breached the door and put several well-aimed rounds into the insurgent, eliminating the threat. The skinny, not so popular, Marine showed poise, courage, and put his brothers above himself. This story stuck with me. I later found out if a recruit makes it through boot camp and earns the title Marine, it doesn't matter how they look. All that matters is how you carry yourself, lead and perform.

Not only was this story a learning experience about two different Marines, it was a reflection on the leadership of our very respected Primary Marksmanship Instructor. He would not have told us this story if he didn't care about us. Sergeant Segura wanted us to succeed and felt it was important for all the recruits and future generations of leaders to hear. Leaders teach you more than the topic at hand, which in our case was marksmanship. Typically, leaders teach you lessons that are important enough to pass down from generation to generation.

"Don't let anyone look down on you because you are young, but set an example for the believers in speech, in conduct, in love, in faith and in purity." (1 Timothy 4:12)

Passenger

Here is an example of a leader who showed many of the previous leadership traits. His name is Todd Beamer and hopefully you already know who he is. The honorable Mr. Beamer was on Flight 93 the morning of September 11, 2001. He made a phone call which recorded a lot of the conversation and actions of the passengers on the plane as they heroically saved hundreds, if not thousands of lives. The hijacked plane was en route to Washington and presumed to have been headed for the Capital or the White House. If successful, the terrorists would have inevitably killed hundreds or thousands of more innocent people. Knowing what had happened with the other three planes and their attacks, Beamer was involved in the plan to attempt to take back control of the plane hijacked by evil terrorists.

Understand that you don't have to be military, a pastor, a doctor, a police officer, or a CEO to be a leader. You can be a passenger on a plane. Mr. Beamer made quite the impact. Wheaton College, in Wheaton, Illinois named one of their buildings the "Todd M. Beamer Center." There is a post office and high school named after him. The term "Let's roll," which he spoke prior to advancing on the terrorists, would later be used as a slogan by the military in Afghanistan, by President Bush, written on Air Force jets, city firetrucks, and on school athletic jerseys. These organizations were following Mr. Beamer's example. However, Mr. Beamer was not the only hero on that flight. There were numerous other heroes on the plane that day.

Fathers, mothers, husbands, wives, pastors, elders, professionals, civil servants, doctors, teachers, siblings, first responders, salespeople, maintenance workers, secretaries. Please pay attention to the good leaders around you. Hopefully when it is your turn, you can help the next man or woman advance up another step.

Society and the workforce

As a young man, I learned a valuable lesson while delivering parcels for a local courier. While holding a package and quickly entering a business, a man in his late 50s or early 60s completely stepped out of my way. I nodded and thanked him, as I wondered why he did that. He looked at me and said, "Never get in the way of a working man," as he motioned with his hand to allow me passage. He truly meant it, and I thought to myself, "What a good rule." I try to apply that rule with the people I run into at work. People coming and going to work get my respect.

A leader's job is to show you how to do it. Your responsibility is to try to do it better when the time is right.

Importance of Leaders. Practical value.

People will bend over backwards for people who have these characteristics. Typically, *good leaders* are well-liked and respected. Good leaders have a chance to show the world what is good. I don't think this should be shocking to anyone, but well-liked people are fun to be around and you want them on your team. Leaders are typically successful. Leaders are winners who stand out in job interviews, and I would argue they make more money in their life.

You will hear some variation of this quote throughout this book but it is worth repeating.

"Winners want other people to win. Losers want other people to lose." - Dave Ramsey

As a business owner, pay attention to resumes as they come across your desk. You might just snag yourself a leader who will take your company to new heights.

Good leaders have an impact on society that cannot be measured.

CHAPTER 18

CONFIDENCE, SELF-WORTH AND IMAGE

The more you win, the more confident you feel. The more knowledgeable you are on a topic, the more confident you will be, especially in your *faith*. With knowledge and confidence comes self-worth. If you are comfortable with your self-worth, you can go on to accomplish great things. You shouldn't feel the pressure to keep up with the Joneses as much as the next guy or girl. If you are confident in yourself, you can honestly ask yourself if you really need a new $100,000 Porsche? Or would you rather save money and be comfortable owning a used Honda or Toyota?

Do not confuse cockiness or arrogance with confidence. I've seen plenty of cocky people stumble and fall. Most of the time arrogant people are the farthest thing from confident, and end up being some of the most self-conscious people I know.

Keep this in mind as you decide what life decisions you are planning for yourself. Confidence is something most anyone can achieve. You will have to cross some waters and obstacles to get there, but even if it is risky or dangerous, you can do it.

This is a picture of the Army Corps of Engineers ferrying one of our convoy's MRAP across the historic Euphrates River.

This could have potentially been a dangerous trip considering we were vulnerable and wide open for an ambush. With all our heavy personal gear, boots, flak jacket, helmet and rifle, if we were attacked it would most likely have been fatal for anyone who fell into the water. However, they got our convoy to where we needed to be quicker, and with less time on the IED laced road, making it worth the risk.

If there is something in your way find a way to get over it, under it, or through it. Don't let obstacles get in your way.

Take a look at this quote by President Ronald Reagan. "Some people spend an entire lifetime wondering if they made a difference in the world. But the Marines don't have that problem."

I'm not saying everyone should join the Marines. My point is, don't just slide through life, live life on purpose. Don't wonder if you made a difference, *know* you made a *difference.* Sometimes you will need to take risks, exit your comfort zone, and go through grueling training or schooling to achieve your goals. My brother earned his PhD in electrical engineering after ten years of post-high school education. My sister became a doctor only by enduring four years of undergraduate college, four years of medical school, three years of Internal Medicine residency, and two years of an Allergy and Immunology fellowship at Mayo Clinic. Thirteen years of training beyond high school. I can't begin to imagine the amount of dedication and patience needed to accomplish each of their goals.

I remember seeing my sister bring stacks and stacks of college textbooks home for spring "break." To me, it appeared to take a lifetime to read all those books, let alone do it all in a week. Needless to say, her spring breaks were a little different from mine, but similar in some respects. We both stayed up late, however she was reading and studying while mine was spent playing beer pong, enjoying my "break" from a long grueling year of playing beer pong, (I am *very grateful* that God revealed a much *better way*.) She got up early to continue studying, I slept in.

This is another reason I don't agree with redistribution of wealth. Why should she work a lot harder than me for over a decade only to be forced (by an entity that has proven to be far below average with finances), to give her money, which she earned by spending sleepless nights studying and training, to someone less *deserving* and not nearly as ambitious? There were some *obvious differences* in our *behaviors*, resulting in some obvious differences in our accomplishments and salaries, and rightfully so. *Prospering* from *hard work* is a *good thing.* The Bible says, *"the laborer is worthy of his hire"* (I Timothy 5:18).

I don't believe my sister has to wonder if she gave it her personal best or made a difference in people's lives. It's the same for my brother. He worked extremely hard to reach the final goal of earning his PhD. He spent many late nights researching and writing his dissertation. Since graduation, he went on to design and test new medical imaging systems, earning numerous patents. He has undoubtedly made a difference in people's lives.

I think of my father who spent seven years volunteering for the local EMS/Fire Department. He doesn't have to worry if he made a difference in his community, he knows he did.

Learn self-defense. Learn a trade. Find faith. Train for and run a marathon. Master a hobby you always wanted to start. Stand up for people who can't or won't stand up for themselves. God doesn't make mistakes. You are a designer's model. He made us the way we are supposed to be. Be who He wants you to be and be confident with who he wants you to be. Even the hairs on your head are numbered. He wants doctors and scientists who work on improving medical devices, and Marines and Soldiers. Ask yourself this question: Are you trying to glorify God with your image, or are you focused on self-glorification? In my opinion, glorifying yourself can cost you a pretty penny. Cars, clothes, and fancy suits are examples of outward appearances that don't make you important. Being made in God's image is what makes you and your neighbor important.

In closing please read this verse:

"But the Lord said to Samuel, 'Do not look on his appearance or on the height of his stature, because I have rejected him. For the Lord sees not as man sees; man looks on the outward appearance, but the Lord looks on the heart.'" (1 Samuel 16:7)

CHAPTER 19

Slow is smooth, smooth is fast. This was a saying we constantly heard in the Marines. Typically, it was said in the context of our learning how to become riflemen and training for combat, but this truism also applies to investing.

I'll walk you through my style of investing, but I'm going to warn you that it's not for everyone. I'm a simpleton and this is what works for me. Averaging eight percent returns annually is successful, however some will argue that it's not the best way to make money.

I'm not day trading or trying to get rich quick. You won't see me using my returns to pay for a car, vacation, or supplement my salary. My returns are reinvested and compounded. I invest for retirement and, in all reality, I hope to never have to touch this money. You could also say this is my retirement rainy day fund. If I decide to use it during retirement, I hope it has something to do with purchasing a lake house or piece of land in the mountains to enjoy with my beautiful wife and children. Hopefully, this turns out to be true, but the main point is, we don't plan on running out of money during retirement. What would be even better is never touching it and saving it for my children or grandchildren's education. What a blessing that would be.

If our retirement fund makes it into our children and grandchildren's hands, I will make sure they know that their inheritance is a blessing they are only enjoying by the good *grace* of God. God taught us and allowed us to be smart with money. "You are benefitting from it because He wants you to benefit, please use it wisely and enjoy it."

Look at what Proverbs 13:22 says. "*Good people leave an inheritance to their grandchildren, but the sinner's wealth passes to the Godly.*" Allow me to say, "Yes I am a sinner," and so are you. I believe what this verse is saying is that sinners who do not repent and stubbornly insist on living in the dark, enjoying their sinful ways, will suffer consequences – and not just financially. Hopefully, we can all agree that bad decisions lead to bad paths. Godly people care about others, especially their grandchildren. You might argue sinners only care about themselves.

So how do I suggest you invest to build wealth? This is what I do. Again, you can decide what you want to do with your money, I am only giving you my personal strategies. If you have a good grasp of the market and want to try your hand a different way, more power to you.

The first lesson of investing is, only invest in something you understand. This applies for all types of investing. Before investing in the stock market, get to know the basics of economics and learn how the market works. When investing in real estate, take time to get to know the local, state, and national housing market. Dave Ramsey taught me this, "The money isn't made in the sale but in the purchase." He was talking about real estate, but this applies to anything and everything when it comes to investing. Buy low, sell high. Common sense, right? Sometimes I feel sense isn't very common these days.

Proverbs 19:2 says, "*Enthusiasm without knowledge is no good, haste makes mistakes.*" Be patient and understand what you are doing. If you are unsure, ask someone you trust for advice and to check your research results. If you need to, seek out a financial advisor. Remember, history always repeats itself.

The second lesson is to actually start the process. If you're new to the market, don't get caught up in trying to find the "perfect" fund. If you've done your research and found a couple decent performing funds that fit for you, do it. The earlier, the better. Hurry up and wait.

Remember, mutual funds and index funds aren't designed to be a get rich quick type of investing. They can make you rich, but for the most part it's because you're allowing the fund to grow and build wealth. Allow compound interest to do most of the heavy lifting. The power behind compound interest is amazing but it does take time. Albert Einstein said, "Compound interest is the eighth wonder of the world. He who understands it, earns it… he who doesn't… pays it." Once it gets its roots set, watch out. This means you college student and recent college grads, start yesterday (only after you have done your due diligence). Proverbs 13:11 reminds us, "*Wealth from get-rich-type schemes quickly disappears, wealth from hard work grows over time.*"

I invest in an S&P 500 index fund. I chose to go this route because I don't have the time or resources to investigate companies and their balance sheets. Personally, I am content and grateful (hopefully you read my grateful chapter) with decent performing index funds. Buying and selling stocks takes a lot of your time and attention, which I don't have. I will gladly accept an average of eight percent annual return on my S&P 500 index fund. It's hands off and I just let it ride. That's my view and you can decide if that's a good method for you and yours. If you can beat the stock market, more power to you. If you get that *hot* tip from a friend and want to run with it, go for it. But if it doesn't pan out the way you hoped, just don't cry over spilled milk, tough guy.

With that being said, the S&P 500 is volatile. There will be years when the value plummets, I'm not going to kid you about that. But on average you will make money in the S&P 500 over the long haul. Warren Buffett was asked how much money he lost during the market crash of 2008. He said, "Nothing, I didn't sell. "That is the time you want to remember your training; be consistent and continue buying. Some people refer to times like that with panic and fear, others calmly refer to it as opportunity. I have a good friend at work who refers to this time as a "buying season."

Watch out for high management fees. With any type of investing, please inquire about the management fees before you commit. Decide what fees you are comfortable with and take time to shop around. I use Vanguard, which is an investment management company. Once I set up an online account with Vanguard, I created a ROTH IRA and purchased a S&P 500 index fund called VFIAX. VFIAX has an expense ratio of only 0.04%. This account is a self-directed Roth individual retirement account (IRA).

There are many different types of IRAs but I decided to use the Roth IRA because its contributions are made after-tax. When I am eventually ready to withdraw this money it will be tax free. I also have a traditional IRA where the contributions are pre-tax, but I'm not currently contributing to it. Each situation is different, but I learned that the Roth will be better in my personal financial situation. I max out my annual contributions to my Roth IRA and let it grow. Since I self-manage my Roth through Vanguard, the management fees are low. There are other self-managed funds and companies out there with low fees, so don't feel obligated to use Vanguard.

Obviously, diversification is also very important. You never want to put all your eggs in one basket. For me, the S&P 500 index is diversified enough. However, we also have shares of Vanguard's small cap exchange traded fund VB. I also use a deferred comp 457 Plan B account set up through my employer. In this account I have six different mutual funds. State or local government employees, public education institutions and tax-exempt organization employees have the option to use a 457 Plan B type of account. This account allows you to invest some of your salary pre-tax and defer paying taxes on the earnings until you withdraw your money. The theory behind this is the money will compound quickly. This account is more or less an experiment to see if I can outperform a professional management company. So far, although they have similar returns, I usually outperform them.

Planning for retirement is a long-term plan and of course there is risk involved. In my opinion you can't time the market. However, if you're going on a four year stretch of solid returns and planning to retire in the near future and *want* to *access* those funds, you might want to consider taking all, or a portion of it out while it's high. Then you can transfer it into something safer like a high yield bond or simply place it in your savings account.

I want to reiterate the importance of compound interest. It is called the eighth wonder of the world, interest on interest. Look at the rule of 72. Divide the rate of return by 72. According to the historical rate of return for my VFIAX fund, I can expect to get right around 8 percent. For example, when I divide 72 by 8, I will double my money in 9 years. See what happens when you double that money a few times. Do a simple internet search for a compound interest calculator. Plug and play and see how the magic works. Hopefully, you take advantage of compound interest. Here is an example of what could happen if someone would have placed $10,000 in the S&P 500 in 1954 then never added another penny to it. As of 2020 you would have $897,938, and all you had to do was let it grow. Imagine if you could figure out a way to add to it monthly. You would be filthy rich.

Remember, I'm not a financial advisor by any means, nor do I claim to be. There are tons of ways to invest but remember, your brain is your best asset. Always invest in yourself. That is truly the most important advice I can give you. That might not be what you want to hear, you might prefer hearing about some magic gimmick, but in my opinion it is true.

Invest in your family first and foremost. Your young kids will never ask, "Hey daddy or mommy, how is your portfolio this quarter?" But I can assure you they will ask, "Mommy where's daddy?" or, "Daddy where's mommy?" My boring eight percent return a year is too shameful to talk with my kids about, but at least they don't have to ask mommy where I'm at because I'm off researching my latest *hot* tip or looking at balance sheets and financial reports. I'm not talking about someone who makes a living off finance, I'm talking about the person who does this with their free/family time. Hopefully, this leaves you with something to think about.

Along with doing your own research, find a mentor or family member you trust, not someone trying to sell you something but someone who cares about your best interests. In my case I was mentored by my brother and father, and they basically taught me everything in this chapter. At my request, I had them look over my work to make sure I was making smart decisions. This gave me peace of mind and helped me get started with my own investing.

One last idea I want you to look at before we move on. Please look at this chart on the S&P 500 index history since 1959. What trend do you see?

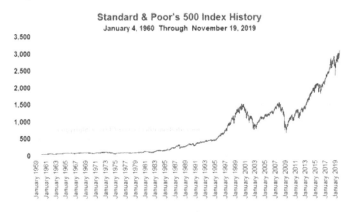

I have lived through two major lows in the market, the 2008 market dip and the COVID-19 low in 2020. They both taught me valuable lessons. Nothing changes.

Don't change your long-term game plan. If you are investing for the long term, don't panic or sell low. Remember what Warren Buffett said when asked about how much money he lost during 2008, "Nothing, I didn't sell."

I wish you good luck trying to time or predict the market during those times. If you can, more power to you. On March 9, 2020 the S&P 500 went down a *historic* 7.6 %. Crazy right?... not really. The way I see it, it was a good time to buy and I bought in at a 7.6 % discount. I was going to buy anyway, so I might as well buy at a discount. I wasn't necessarily trying to time the market, I was *reacting* to it. The next day it went up approximately 5%. I didn't panic during this time. During the big panic, I didn't sell a *single* share. After the S&P 500 went down drastically, it took approximately three short months to recover. During this time, I added *significantly* more shares to our portfolio and our net worth went up *drastically*.

CHAPTER 20

VACATIONS

Before kids, we traveled whenever we had the chance. Aruba for our honeymoon, Puerto Rico, The Big Island of Hawaii, and California. Although we spent a decent amount of money, we always planned ahead and found good deals. We really enjoyed seeing the world *together* and experiencing God's creation. That being said, I don't miss it as much as I thought I would. At this point in my life, I would much rather drive the family to Wisconsin or Michigan to enjoy a weekend at the beach for a fraction of the cost. Traveling has always been a passion of ours, and it is also one of the reasons we save money now. Travel has taken a back seat to raising our children.

We learned vacations don't make you happy, they are just a short escape from reality. Instead of escaping, make your reality happy. Don't get me wrong, vacations are meaningful but planning and staying within your means are more important. When the kids are grown and we have financial freedom, we plan to drive across the country and allow the wind to take us wherever it pleases. Hopefully, we will visit every state and see the best that each has to offer. This won't be possible if we aren't in a good financial position.

Learning what delayed gratification means is something that helped me in life, including our finances. Vacations are for people who can afford them. If you're going into debt to go on vacation, you should reconsider. If you can afford taking a vacation: do your homework, plan ahead, and stay on budget. If you want a bargain don't get stuck in an over-crowded tourist area. The most fun we had while on vacation were those times we found ourselves off the beaten path and far from the touristy areas.

About seven years ago, my wife and I were fortunate enough to go on a dream vacation to the Big Island of Hawaii. Honestly, this isn't the most glamorous island. It's known for its natural beauty, lower cost of living and laid-back atmosphere. Before even deciding to go, we researched and planned the whole trip to see if it was feasible financially. I bought a used book about the Big Island and began planning months in advance. We also had lots of helpful advice from my brother and his wife who have been to Hawaii numerous times. Luckily, it was feasible because we took in some amazing sights. We saw green sand beaches, black sand beaches, white sand beaches, salt and pepper beaches, waterfalls, mountains, volcanoes, sea turtles, beautiful valleys, and the most beautiful ocean water imaginable. We swam with manta rays and dolphins.

Our most memorable experience was snorkeling in Honaunau Bay with approximately thirty wild spinner dolphins within three feet of us. That will be a memory I'll never forget. All the sites I just mentioned didn't charge admission fees, except for the manta ray tour. We spent a little under $3,000 for this trip. We stayed 10 days on the island, rented a car, flew from Chicago, flew from the Big Island to Oahu to see Pearl Harbor, and paid for food. Unbelievable, right?

This trip was prior to having children and my views on debt and finance have since changed drastically. I will show you what we did, even though I disagree with this credit card strategy now and don't recommend it. (Credit cards can be very harmful. They give you a good excuse to overspend, which can quickly spiral to out of control debt). To pay for our flights, which would've been around $1,200 each, we each signed up for a credit card to use the miles. Let me be clear, we didn't carry any debt on the cards and paid them in full the moment we got the bill. In our case, we didn't pay a cent in interest. We saved around $2,400 in air fare alone. We are very disciplined with our finances and bills, but I won't do this again. Luckily, it worked out for us. If we weren't able to get the flights for free, I don't think we would have gone.

I estimate we spent an average of $135 a night on hotels. We spent $550 on flights, bus fare and admission to Pearl Harbor. A modest rental car was $450. We went to the local grocery store, not in the touristy area, to purchase cereal and lunch items. We spent around $50 on groceries which made up approximately 10 meals. When we went out for dinner, we usually split a meal and it wasn't uncommon for our total to be under $30 with tip and tax. Gas was around $100. The Manta Ray tour was $250 total.

For a wedding gift, our friend, who was a flight attendant, gave us free flights. This blessing allowed us to see the whole island of Puerto Rico. Because of this gift, we were able to complete the trip for a very reasonable price. We utilized the same strategies in Hawaii and stayed off the beaten path. We did our research and discovered an island off the coast of Puerto Rico called Vieques. It has secluded beaches that are straight out of a postcard. Vieques has a bio bay that is fluorescent at night with wild horses, snorkeling and a quaint hotel. The inn we stayed at had a beautiful view of the ocean, an infinity pool, bar and restaurant, outdoor lobby, all on a secluded twenty-acre property.

From what I remember, there are only two places to stay on the island. A large resort that cost around $400 a night or this small hotel for around $100 a night. We aren't the big resort types anyway, and I'm glad we got the real experience of Vieques at this quaint hotel while also paying a lot less. This is what I envision parts of Heaven looking like, and it helps me stay on track for my Christian walk.

This was also the case for our California trip. We rented a car and drove from San Diego to San Jose to Napa Valley to Yosemite to Mammoth, then back to San Diego. The most enjoyable sights we saw did not charge admission. The relaxing waters of Los Osos, Morro Bay and China Cove were amazing. There were elephant seals soaking up the sun on the beach, just steps from the Pacific Coast Highway.

This image is McWay Falls, an 80-foot waterfall in Julia Pfeiffer Burns State Park. McWay Falls is in the Big Sur area of California, about 35 miles south of Carmel. This was one of our more memorable views during our trip.

We saw seals swimming in the bay off Fisherman's Wharf in Monterey, California. The breath-taking views of Yosemite's mountainsides, waterfalls, and endless scenes of nature were free. We saw dolphins swimming in the distance off the beaches of Carlsbad and Oceanside while soaking up the sun. We drove by Marine Corps base Camp Pendleton and toured MCRD San Diego as a visitor. The most expensive part of the trip was Napa Valley with its very expensive lodging and restaurants. In our opinion, it was a waste of time and completely overrated. The whole area is based on tourism and consumerism. You can feel it. What I'm trying to say is, you can have a ton of fun without paying the big bucks. Plan ahead, do your research, have a budget, and don't get stuck in a tourist trap.

I know a lot of people do not want to want to hear this, but if you are *broke* you should not go on expensive trips. Stay local and visit a park while attacking debt. There are typically plenty of low-cost sites to see locally. Lake Michigan beaches in the summer are just as much fun as any beach on earth. Vacation is time to get away from it all, right? Maybe you wouldn't need to get away if you had certain aspects of your life under control, including your finances. Spending family time together should be the most important part of the vacation. The upside is, you don't need to fly your family halfway across the world to spend time *together*.

CHAPTER 21

FOOD AND BEVERAGE

If you have taken my previous advice and dissected your spending, hopefully you noted how much you spend on food. We need food to survive, I'm sure we all agree on that. But do you realize how much you are actually spending when you leave the grocery store or restaurant? It can get quite expensive. I freely admit, I had been awful at spending on food for most of my life. I saw it as a need and didn't really care how much I spent. Naturally, I wanted to see how I could improve that. But this meant I had to change my mindset.

I started looking into why food costs so much. There are a lot of different people involved in the production and handling of food. Farmers, food prep, packaging, salespeople, shipping-delivery, unloading, shelving, etc. Food is big business because there will always be a need. The way our culture is currently, there will always be a need for convenience. This need for convenience drives up the cost of prepackaged food. As a society, we want meals that are ready to eat and only take three minutes to prepare in the microwave. Mothers and fathers are working long hours. Throw in sports, band, and church in the mix, and it's very clear why convenience sells.

A few years ago, my co-workers and I decided to bring our lunches to work instead of eating out. This saved me approximately $75 a week. Those savings really added up over time.

My wife, who loves to cook, makes a large batch of red beans and rice then freezes them in individual sized meals, ready to bring to work each day. She estimates that each meal costs less than 75 cents. She does the same for chili, pulled pork, and numerous other dishes I like.

She purchases the type of food that heats up well with no discernible difference in taste after freezing. All the meals listed above cost under a dollar a meal, home cooked and filling. I can also control the portion size and not overeat like I do at most restaurants.

Another suggestion would be to plant some vegetable and fruit bushes. These are relatively cheap to plant and easy to maintain. You won't save yourself thousands, but you will save a couple dollars here and there. Having a garden is beneficial in many ways. You become more self-reliant and you know what you are eating. You are also personally invested in the outcome of the produce (care and watering). I plan on teaching the kids how it all works, which will pay off in a non-financial way. Hopefully, my boys will have a "can do attitude" when they become men.

I'm not a morning person and I often skipped making a home-cooked breakfast. We used to buy breakfast bowls that heat up in the microwave for convenience that cost about $2.50 each. My wife decided she was tired of overpaying for something she could make for a lot cheaper and decided to make them from scratch. She batches them out and freezes them individually. Total cost: About 50 cents a meal. You need time and have to be prepared, but it saves us money. Being prepared will not only save you stress in life, it will also save you money.

It is unreal the amount of money people spend on coffee. It's safe to say some people spend over five dollars a day at their favorite coffee shop. I refuse to spend that for a single cup of coffee. My wife makes our own at the house. She can buy a whole bag of coffee for around five dollars and it will last us at least two weeks. At the most it costs 50 cents a cup, and that is a generous estimation. Let's calculate how much some people spend on coffee each month by multiplying five by thirty. It comes out to about $150 a month. What if you placed that money in a decent performing mutual fund? If you did, you would see what compound interest can do for you. If you achieve a seven percent yearly average return, which is easily attainable, you would have roughly $113,848.27 after 25 years of investing.

Be prepared and use your time wisely--it will pay off substantially.

CHAPTER 22

When I lost my mom, my world changed. My body was mentally, emotionally, and physically exhausted. I felt like my body was in shock. This was my first taste of death of that magnitude, and I hope to never go through it again. Unfortunately, we all know this is not reality. I couldn't imagine going through a loss like that if she was my main provider.

I remind my wife there is nothing I can do to help when I am gone. I can't get a second job or take on some overtime if we are down on our luck financially. Do you want your significant other to be forced to deal with such a horrible loss along with all the expenses it entails while simultaneously worrying about finances? If I were to die today my wife would receive well over a million dollars. I estimate she could raise our kids for at least 20 years with that. She would not "need" to remarry, go back to school, or work a job right away. The money would help her get back on her feet and she would not be forced to adjust to any more life-changing events. I can promise you that your world will be in shambles and turned upside down when this happens. Don't add to the mess by not being *prepared* financially. Get a decent life insurance policy. Figure out how much it will cost your family to live comfortably for an entire year with that being their only source of income. Then take that number and multiply it by how many years you want to provide for them. For example, $75,000 a year times 20 years is 1.5 million dollars. Remember, life insurance benefits are not taxed, making it a great benefit.

There are two options, Whole Life and Term Life. Don't take my word for it and do your own research regarding what I am about to say. Prior to meeting with my insurance agent, my Dad gave me some advice. He taught me the basics of whole life and term insurance and warned me that agents will try and sell me whole life because it makes them the most money, not because it is better for the client. I did some research along with my dad's two cents, and common sense won. In my opinion, term is the best option. Just give my wife a check if it comes to that. I don't need your investing help or to keep up with your "cash value" idea. If you took the money you saved by avoiding whole life and invested the amount in an index fund or mutual fund, you will come out way ahead. Index funds have much greater returns and lower fees than whole life plans. That is the name of the game.

CHAPTER 23

CAREERS, SALARIES AND SIDE JOBS

Keep this in mind as you are deciding on a career; income is your biggest wealth building asset.

With that in mind, please don't forget, one of the biggest themes in this book is that money doesn't buy happiness. However, the career you choose is important in the eyes of your Creator, and important to His people. Here are some ideas to ponder when deciding on which career route to take: Will this career help God's people, or is it only about me? Or both?

Is this something I will enjoy for an extended period of time? Am I drawn to this profession strictly for the money? John 3:27 warns, "*A person cannot receive even one thing unless it is given to him from heaven.*" Will I be able to raise a family on the salary? Will I need to go into a large amount of debt to achieve a degree in this field? Will the salary match the debt ratio?

Will I please God with the profession I choose? Revelation 3:7, "*What he opens no one can shut, what he shuts no one can open.*" Is this profession right for me? "*The purpose of a person's heart are deep waters, but one who has insight draws them out*" (Proverbs 20:5). Is this a good profession if I am married and/or with kids? "*Put your outdoor work in order and get your fields ready; after that, build your house*" (Proverbs 24:27).

If you could do anything in the world, what would it be? Then ask yourself, is this feasible and what would I need to do to make that happen? There are many countries in the world where these questions cannot be asked. Communist/Socialist countries make those kinds of dreams mute. Always have confidence in your abilities and future abilities. You can learn something new if you want to. Are you hungry? Yes, I could eat. Are you starving? I am *going* to *find* a *way* to eat. How bad do you want it?

I found thousands of articles about millionaires that show they have multiple sources of income. A CNBC.com article, *4 things Millionaires do that the middle class doesn't* – published by Emmie Martin stuck out to me the most. The reason I chose this article is due to her teaching style and wording. One of the points she makes is: Millionaires *cultivate* multiple sources of income. *Cultivate.* The article gives a great example of a fisherman who only casts a single line versus a fisherman with five lines cast. Who is going to catch more fish? Simple explanation.

If you have a hobby or skill you enjoy, consider cultivating it into another source of income. For years I wanted to try my hand at woodworking. I wanted to be challenged, practice patience, and make something out of nothing. I decided to make hand-carved wooden American flags. I bought a used table saw and dove in. I did my research and shopped around and found good deals. I found ads on Craigslist for free wood. For under $250 I bought a rotary tool, saw, and wood clamps. This opened a door to a whole different world. I learned a lot about tools and what it means to be a craftsman. My dad taught me some basics, and I learned more advanced techniques online. There are plenty of people who want others to win posting advice and techniques online. Woodworking takes a lot of man hours and is the opposite of a passive form of income, but what was more important than the money was that I invested in myself. I learned a lot about people, sales, and marketing. I now have the tools and skills to start something from the ground up. I did it once, and I *can do* it *again* if need be.

If your sole purpose is to make money with your side job, find a passive income source. Passive income is income you earn that doesn't take up a great deal of your precious time or thoughts. Mutual funds, index funds, stocks, dividends, royalties, building an app, sometimes real estate or being a silent business partner can all be examples of ways to cultivate passive income. *Real* millionaires utilize these passive income tools to build wealth. At a certain point, millionaires' careers simply become – being a millionaire.

I made a couple of dollars with my flag hobby, and most of it went directly to my children's custodial UTMA (Uniform Transfers to Minor Act) account. I bought the fund VB, which is Vanguards Small Cap index fund, Exchange Traded Fund (ETF). Small Caps are funds composed of small caps within an index. Small Caps are volatile, however over long periods they typically produce high returns. Small Caps are good options for long-term investing. Luckily for my children, we started this account when they were all under the age of six. When they get old enough, I will show them how it works, creating a wonderful opportunity for them to learn.

If you enjoy making wood flags, for example, and want to expand your business to full time, don't quit your day job. Make them on the side and perfect them. Once you have perfected them, *take over the market* as the best flag builder in the world or *die trying.* In my opinion, these should be your only two options. If you want it, fight for it tooth and nail.

Throw it at the wall and see what sticks. If what you are doing isn't a good fit, try another method. Read a book on marketing. Ask a successful business owner how they did it. Read Proverbs. A wise businessman recommended reading Proverbs, which he claimed was one of the most important books for a businessman to read. After reading Proverbs, I absolutely agree.

Can you support a family comfortably with the career you choose? If you cannot support your family, you have failed. We aren't cultivating failures. If you failed at your dream, don't quit. It is a temporary situation. It is a sign you will have to work harder and longer for it. Delayed gratification is something successful people have mastered. It might take time, maybe a decade, but if you want it then *do* it. Get formal training, self-learn, pick the brains of successful people who have done it.

"*Ask* [and keep on asking] *and it will be given to you; seek* [and keep on seeking] *and you will find; knock* [and keep on knocking] *and it will be opened for you.*" (Matthew 7:7)

CHAPTER 24

"For even the Son of Man came not to be served but to serve others and to give his life as a ransom for many." (Mark 10:45)

Being a servant involves having a mindset that changes one's thinking. With this mindset of servant leadership, you begin seeing the needs of others while continually learning that the world doesn't revolve around you. Service for the right reasons will benefit many.

A while back I was patrolling with my assigned police partner for the day. We observed two well-known teenagers loitering in an area known for having numerous problems – armed robberies, burglaries, and thefts. One of the kids fled the second he caught sight of us. I exited and chased him on foot until he was eventually caught by a responding officer. I had a long talk with him that day. I have sadly learned that these talks rarely have any effects on these kids, but I never give up trying. I told him bad decisions will always lead to bad paths and bad lifestyles. I informed him how important his choices are, and to start making some better ones today.

About four years later, this same young man was murdered. My talks with him didn't appear to have helped, and it was hard to bear. After his homicide I heard rival gang members taunting his mother and brother about the murder. If that's not pure evil, I don't know what is. A couple years later, our Police Department was able to assist another jurisdiction just minutes after a shooting where we located one of the "taunters" who was the offender in this current shooting.

We knew about a personal beef between these two and had a good idea where the offenders were going in our jurisdiction. We were correct, and I was able to personally put the handcuffs on the taunter mentioned above. Thankfully, he is still in prison for the shooting. He knew he was done for, defeated. On a normal day he also flagrantly taunted police officers. But what do you think I did when I arrested him that day? I treated him with respect, even though in my flesh I didn't want to. Ironically, this was the only time in his life when he was respectful toward me. While it felt good knowing we were able to take a bad guy off the street, more importantly, we knew we were serving that taunted mother who lost her son to street violence. Sometimes serving is not doing everything you want to do, but instead doing what you should do.

Sadly, this was not the only person murdered after our department tried to help him. In fact, a person was murdered about thirty feet away from where the two of us once had a 45-minute conversation about life. I let him speak and he let me speak. At the beginning of the conversation there were times we both raised our voices. I remember asking if he was ever taught right from wrong, and he didn't like that very much. He responded by blaming the police for giving him a felony, which he claimed prevented him from getting a job (even though he also told me he couldn't work due to arthritis in his thumb, and he had *more* than *one* felony).

We didn't agree on everything but the conversation was civil, and towards the end he knew I was trying to help. By the way, I arrested him about three times prior to this conversation. As we wound things down, he started to look me in the eyes, which he previously refused to do. This told me he was listening to what I had to say. During part of the conversation God came up, and I mentioned that I believed in Him and he referenced God too. I informed him that, if what he was telling me was true (his faith and if he repented), one day there would be a good chance we could be friends, and hopefully I wouldn't have to chase him around anymore. He smiled because we both knew he ran from me a couple times before. This person normally didn't like the police and refused to have anything to do with us. Unfortunately, he was a very angry man.

After this conversation, my future contacts with him and his friends were completely different. If one of his friends started taunting me, he told them to be quiet, that I was only doing my job.

His tragic murder helped some people see us as "people" and not just "police." There were prayer vigils and peace walks that my partner and I attended. At one point we found ourselves in the victim's apartment, holding hands and praying with his grandparents, cousins, and friends. They weren't strangers to me, as I had arrested a few of them before. This sad event was used by God to bring the police and citizens together because through this incident they came to see a different side of us. They now realized we truly cared about them and their community. We could have stayed back and just been content providing security, but we didn't. We participated on our own accord.

A couple years later I attended a monthly community event in the same area. This meeting had more people in attendance than normal due to the recent shooting death of a teenage girl. Emotions were high and citizens brought up issues in this open group discussion. Naturally, people tended to blame and direct their anger towards us. One citizen asked what we were doing to keep kids away from street life and why we didn't mentor kids in the neighborhood. My first thought was, we actually do try to help kids, but unfortunately most of the time they ignore us. You can lead a horse to water, but you can't make him drink – but that doesn't stop us from keep trying. If I can reach one, I have helped. Second thought I had was, how *terribly wrong* this citizen *confused* police and *parental roles*. I was shocked.

Out of respect for the grieving community and grieving mother, I calmly explained to everybody that we do our best to mentor kids when we get the chance. In fact, I had a conversation with the Urban Youth Ministry Program coordinator a few days before this young girl's death about ways to help her. We both agreed that the first person who saw or talked to her would ask if she would be willing to have a talk with both of us to see how we could help. Unfortunately, she died before we saw her again. The youth leader had her in some of their summer camps and activities. She saw a lot of potential in her and thought she would do really well if she got some help, love and attention. In the meeting I didn't say anything about how we tried to help the young girl (mostly because the mother of the girl was present for the meeting), but I did mention the conversation I had with the victim I spoke of earlier. This was a close-knit community, so they all knew who I was referring to.

I informed them that I mentored him for almost an hour within feet of where he was murdered less than a year later. I mentioned tidbits of our conversation and info only someone close to him would know to show them all I wasn't blowing smoke. I mentioned how he had plans of playing pro ball in Europe. I shared with the group how I advised him to go out and achieve his goals. "You won't make Europe if you are out there acting like a fool, smoking weed and drinking all day. You need to train." I also shared my calling him out during this conversation when I pointed out I had never seen him with a basketball in my life. I told him I would personally go to the basketball court with him if that would help.

I knew the impact he could have on this community, and I wanted to see him excel and change. There were rumors that he was the leader of the local gang. I told the group that despite all my best efforts, he never took my advice and I never saw him improving his basketball ability. When I told the group he never took me up on my offer to go to the court with him, everyone went quiet and you could hear a pin drop.

What happened next was amazing. I have learned in life that people need to hear the truth and being politically correct is usually more harmful than open honesty. My words opened up the discussion and more members of the community started talking freely. Local residents I thought would never say anything positive about the police stood up to speak in front of the group. They informed other citizens that I was a good guy and one to be trusted. Remember, these were the same people who previously would not even dream of speaking to the police over anything, let alone praise our work. Instead, they now trusted the police after seeing our genuine service.

It has been said, "people want to know how much you care before they care how much you know." I always had the mindset that this was not only their community, but my community as well. I think they began to see that. I had been assigned to this district and community for over seven years. I take responsibility for the area and my goal is to leave it better than I found it.

I have been fortunate to serve alongside many police officers who also take their service to the community seriously. One summer day we received a call for an accident with injuries in a residential area. The caller(s) relayed that the hit and run offender was running from the scene and it looked like a bad accident. Numerous officers responded. Upon arrival, I saw a woman ejected from the van lying next to a fire hydrant, unable to get up. I later learned she landed on the fire hydrant and her injuries were gruesome. Thankfully, she miraculously survived. Another passenger, most likely the grandmother, had a severe injury on her forehead. I observed an officer gently holding her hand and being very attentive to her needs, saying soothing words like, "It will be okay. I am here for you. Help is on the way." Fortunately, everyone survived the accident. I will never forget the gruesome injuries that day, but I will also always remember that officer genuinely caring for the injured woman – a stranger to him. I am sure she will never forget it either.

Our tour of duty in Iraq was not exactly what I had envisioned, but we served the country well. Our MAP conducted over one hundred and fifty combat missions and traveled over 10,000 miles in a Mine Resistance Armor Protected. Our average speed was between 15 to 25 mph, which required patience. I'm not complaining because being in the back of the MRAP was a safe place to be. Marines, soldiers, airmen, and sailors didn't have that luxury earlier in the war. They were forced to weld steel plates and makeshift armor to their Humvees until the MRAPs were deployed to the fleet. I often thought about the pressure the driver and vehicle commander shouldered on all our missions. They had to be alert and keep their head on a swivel every second, scanning for danger. Same for the machine gunners in the turret where temperatures can easily reach up to 150 degrees. They had the most important job in the convoy because they were in charge of arguably the most impactful weapon we have. I'm thankful for their service and being an integral part of the team.

Orphan and class clowns

I had a teacher in high school who was raised in an orphanage. If you asked to borrow the stapler on his desk – he would say, "No, you can't borrow the stapler." And he would then tuck it away in his desk. Or he would say something like, "I was an orphan, get your own;" or "I never had anything of my own. This is mine." He would walk the halls with his hard heavy briefcase and bang the smart alecks or class clowns in the thigh with it. I will never forget the look of contentment on his face after scoring a direct hit. He always said the worst part about teaching is watching the kids getting progressively worse over the years.

This was his way of getting back. He was not a jerk, even though he looked like one on the surface. He taught at the school for many years and only one graduating class asked him to speak at graduation. I think this was because most of the classes assumed he would say no. It was rumored by someone close to him that he cried after being asked to speak. He didn't do a disservice by denying us the use of his stapler or pen. He actually did us a service because his actions taught us the need to be prepared and get our own.

Pastor Mark has served five different churches over a period of forty years. Raising a family of seven on a pastor's salary must have been tricky at times. He lived by the many principles I talked about and he taught me a lot about finances. Mark has been the senior pastor at our current church for about fifteen years.

Just recently, we merged with another church. As is common for church mergers, some people decided to leave. After two years, the church members realized we couldn't afford to keep all the pastors. Mark is 68 and he and Cindy have been smart with their finances. They invested, stayed out of debt, and are now receiving social security.

Because of their financial situation, he offered to take a fifty percent pay cut to keep the rest of the staff in place. Mark and Cindy did this because they believe in disciples making disciples. He could have said, "I have been here the longest, I am the senior pastor, and I will not take a pay cut." Or he could have proposed everyone take an equal pay cut, but he didn't do any of these things. Cindy and Mark decided to sacrifice for the church, the congregation, and his fellow pastors. The elders countered Mark's offer and talked him into taking a twenty-five percent cut, which would give the congregation an opportunity to trust God. The church rose to the challenge and our finances have been solid – even in the midst of a declared pandemic.

My Dad worked long hours and picked up a second job on the weekends, enabling my Mom to stay home and raise the kids. Being a mom isn't a job, but for lack of better terms, it is the toughest job in the world. He also volunteered for a lot of church events including security, ushering, trustees, diaconate, reading Scripture, and decorating the church around Christmas time. His other place of voluntary service is at Wayside Cross Mission, where he mentors people recently released from prison or fighting an addiction.

There's the door

"You don't get it." This was a favorite saying of one of my high school teachers named Doc. Doc served in Vietnam with the Marines. Most of us will never understand the things he saw over there, and I can understand his frustration at seeing all these snotty nosed, bratty kids – "not getting it." He was not talking about the academic lesson he was teaching the class. It was the big picture of life and how things work that most concerned him. He made a point to tell us that we "don't get it," so we would try to get it. He had something to teach us, and he wanted us to learn it. He would sometimes throw the chalk across the room in frustration.

He was also our high school soccer coach. According to a major sports network, his teams ranked nationally in the top twenty for a number of career wins. He treated us all the same, did not play favorites, and worked us hard. I can remember doing bear crawls from goal to goal in scorching heat; not because he was mean but because he wanted us to be tough and mean. He created a winning culture.

Our senior year we had 22 wins, 3 ties and 3 losses. The taste of winning is still something I rely on at times. Winning is a good feeling. By the way, since he retired, the soccer program has been the laughingstock of our conference.

He was well known for telling a disruptive and out of control kid in his history class, "There is the door. You don't wanna be here, do you? You are sixteen, you do not have to be here. You can leave, get up and leave, there is the door." Or he would pull the desk and kid to the front of the class and say, "Everyone stop and look at Jerry. Jerry needs attention so everyone look at him."

It worked. Jerry never left the class and kept his mouth shut. This was the only classroom where he didn't act out. A lot of guys complained about him, but I always liked him. Everyone was treated the same way. I understood him a lot better after arriving at Marine Corps boot camp. Everything he did was for a reason, which is Boot Camp 101.

Dedication

While working as a police officer, I met a gentleman by the name of Fernando. He approached us while on patrol, asking about the possibility of our having a pickup game of soccer with some kids he coached. As I got to know Fernando, I learned he was a former police officer in Mexico who had been through a lot during his time there. Many years ago, Fernando and his cousins refused to meet cartel demands to release some of their top members who were in police custody. They were all kidnapped, shot, and left for dead. The others all died, and Fernando was in a coma for two months but ultimately survived.

Fernando was the only youth FIFA soccer coach in Illinois. He had to complete a very competitive class in Brazil to be certified. Fernando failed the first three times. Before the fourth attempt, he prayed and requested God to use him. This time Fernando passed, allowing him to start a youth soccer team where he volunteers and mentors young players.

Fernando has had an immeasurable impact on his community. He is very proud of serving the kids in the neighborhood. This is all volunteer work, and he does it to serve. He is also very proud of one of his former players who received a full ride soccer scholarship to Villanova, a very expensive and prestigious university. The kid's parents were left speechless at the news.

Arrow Flight 1285

I met Henry in 2019. He was a US Army Soldier in the 1980s and spoke to a group of police officers about Crisis Intervention Training (CIT) and mental illness. In 1985, Henry was picked by his superior to be on the advance party back to America from a deployment in Egypt. Henry was surprised at this request, as he was the only Sergeant in the supply platoon able to handle the movement and shipping of all the supplies. Henry refused to go on the advance party and even addressed his concerns to his higher ups.

They all agreed that Henry was the only one capable of such a task. However, after much begging his superior ultimately won the debate. Henry was sent back with the advance party. Henry still cannot find an explanation for why he was sent back before the rest of his battalion.

The day the main body was supposed to arrive home, December 12, 1985, Henry received news that changed his life forever. Arrow Air Flight 1285 that was carrying the rest of his battalion crashed in Canada, killing all 256 people on board. Henry was placed in charge of sorting the personal gear, labeled with his friends' and brothers' names after it all arrived in Fort Campbell. Henry was also tasked with standing guard and preventing members of the media from sneaking in and taking pictures of the caskets of his fallen brothers. Henry developed severe depression and PTSD over this. He went on to use drugs and hit rock bottom many times before finally getting the help he needed. Henry is now clean and works for NAMI where he mentors and helps hundreds of people with mental illnesses. Henry is a Christian and uses his faith to mentor others and lead by example. He is a special man and Henry inspired me personally in many ways. When he spoke to our CIT class, there wasn't a single person in the room who wasn't moved by his words. God is definitely using Henry and He chose him to be a survivor for a reason. I'm confident his life story will impact anyone who reads it. This type of story is not something you will read about in the news, but I'm committed to telling his story and those of others like him. His desire to help others with mental illness is very honorable, and I am proud to know a servant like him.

Rags, riches and ecosystems

If you haven't seen the film *Mully*, you need to. Charles Mully is a former orphan turned wealthy businessman from Kenya, Africa. He is a true rags to riches story, but that is not the most amazing aspect of his life. After finding purpose in life and a desire to help orphans in Kenya, even against the wishes of his family, he set aside his luxurious life to help kids with no family or hope.

It might be hard to understand the magnitude of what an orphan goes through in Kenya until you see it for yourself. Orphans are seen sleeping in the filthy streets. Mully and his family, who also embraced his decision to renounce wealth, went on to help thousands of orphans. Mully feeds, houses, and provides material needs for his new family of thousands. Working together, they have built housing, dug wells, and planted over a million trees on their property. He puts complete trust in the Lord, and complete confidence that all people are God's children. His service to his community is something that is immeasurable. After you view *Mully*, think about how one person yielding to God was able to change a culture, thousands of people, and an ecosystem. With the million trees that he planted and water from the wells in a desert area, he was literally able to change the local ecosystem. Amen.

Affairs in order

A few years back, my policing unit became involved in a shooting while conducting an undercover detail. During this incident two of my fellow officers in an unmarked vehicle were shot at by gang members. My partner and I were also in plainclothes and in an unmarked vehicle. We were close to the initial scene and heard the gunshots. We responded quickly and found ourselves in the middle of an active gun battle. My supervisor wrote the following in my yearly review, "Ofc James rushed to the aid of his fellow officers and engaged the subject in gunfire. The subject was taken into custody

FIGHT FOR IT FINANCIAL

and none of our officers were injured. Ofc James did not hesitate to assist fellow officers in a chaotic, dangerous situation."

Numerous other officers rushed to their aid as well. I can't speak for the other officers, but Deuteronomy 31:6 means a lot to me, "*Be strong and courageous. Do not be afraid or terrified because of them, for the Lord your God goes with you; He will never leave you nor forsake you.*"

The reason I added this incident is to demonstrate how my faith, loyalty to my fellow officers, love of my family, and financial peace got me through that dangerous ordeal. Before I leave for work, I always tell my family that I love them, which I sincerely do, and kiss them. I never leave without letting them know that. I know where I am going when I die, and I know where my wife is going when she dies. I also know that when I leave for work – if I don't come back – my wife and family will be financially taken care of for decades. We have financial freedom, and we don't carry any debt. We own our house, along with other assets, and she will receive a large sum of money from life insurance. All these things give me *peace* of *mind*. I don't have to worry about the stressful financial noise in my head when I need to be *sharp* while serving.

Be willing to sacrifice while serving

As my partner and I cautiously walked the stairwells of an apartment complex, trying to locate a bad guy with multiple felony warrants, we heard the voice of one of the officers in our unit call out a foot pursuit a few blocks from us. We soon heard the distinct sounds of gunshots over the radio as the officer called in more details of the incident.

~ 173 ~

We later learned that the bad guy was shooting at our officer as he was trying to escape. The officer returned fire but temporarily lost sight of the suspect. We responded and arrived to where the criminal dropped out of sight. Four of us, friends from the same unit, checked on our coworker in the dark alley where he quickly briefed us. I remember checking him for bullet holes, just to make sure his adrenaline didn't cloud any physical injuries.

As I was searching for wounds, we heard the most chilling bloodcurdling scream from a woman you could possibly imagine. I knew it was a mother from the scream alone. It was filled with fear and anger. Without hesitation we ran towards the scream and observed the bad guy standing in the doorway of the lady's house, facing away from us. It appeared she pushed him out of the house but the struggle continued as he was still attempting to enter. As we raced over, I could see her determination was paying off. Not only had this man shot at a police officer, he just committed an armed home invasion on an innocent family.

If you have made it this far in my book you know families are very important to me. This evil bad guy needed to be stopped, and the lady and her family urgently needed help. I remember thinking as I ran towards them, bullets are going to fly my way, but the faster I run the harder it will be to stop me. With my momentum I will get to him whether I'm shot or not. Police are *protectors* and *we were willing* to *prove* it. We needed to protect this family who I instantly felt intimate with the moment I heard her scream.

Protecting this family was our only job, and at this point nothing else mattered. It appeared the other officers were thinking the same thing because they were coming from around the detached garage at full speed. One officer was able to throw the suspect off the concrete steps, freeing the lady from the bad guy. This was all done while he was *holding* the *gun* which *fired* the *shots directly* over the *officer's head* 45 *seconds earlier*. Being surrounded, he decided to take his own life before justice could be served. The officers risked their lives to take a bad guy off the street, essentially taking on the violent armed shooter so someone else didn't have to.

***

Tragically, one of the biggest fears of a police officer occurred in our jurisdiction when an evil person shot and killed five coworkers and shot another person at his place of employment. Out of respect for the victims and their families I will not mention names, but my fellow police officers and our community will never forget them. What I ask is that you pray for the families and friends whose lives will never be the same after that day.

During this incident, five of our police officers were also shot while responding to the threat and helping the wounded. These officers displayed exceptional courage and exemplified what it means to serve their fellow man. There were many heroic acts on that terrible day. We can all make a difference, whether in police work, medical field, garbage man, plumber, landscaper, secretary, pilot, an engineer, or whatever it is. If you do your job in an honorable and positive manner you will have an impact on this world. Don't underestimate the importance of what you can do. The Commander in Chief of the United States of America had this to say about our department, the victims, and their families that day, "Good job by law enforcement in Illinois today. Heartfelt condolences to all of the victims and their families. America is with you."

The reason I decided to talk about this tragic incident is to show the impact a "normal person" can have by simply going to work and doing what they were trained to do. The officers' mission was to help people in need and protect life, which they were willing to do at any cost. Needless to say, they made an *impact* during their *service* to *our community*, our department, our families and our nation.

Romans 12:6-10 says, "*We have different gifts, according to the grace given us. If a man's gift is . . . serving, let him serve; if it is teaching, let him teach; if it is encouraging, let him encourage; if it is contributing to the needs of others, let him give generously; if it is leadership, let him govern diligently; if it is showing mercy, let him do it cheerfully. Don't just pretend to love others. Really love them. Hate what is wrong. Hold tightly to what is good. Love each other with genuine affection, and take delight in honoring each other.*"

If you find yourself at a point in your life where you are wondering what career path you should take or what your gifts and skills are, ask yourself if you have a servant's heart. You may not even realize if you do or don't because you might be a natural "servant," someone who just instinctively gravitates to servanthood. I have worked service jobs since I first started in the workforce at the age of 11, making $3 an hour doing yard work, planting trees and assisting with installing a pond for a landowner in my town.

I bought my first car, erased student loans, paid for a wedding/honeymoon, and paid our house off – strictly from service earnings. This is an attainable niche and skill that will take you, your community, and your family many places.

Conclusion

Hopefully you have picked up on the major themes running throughout this book. Being good with money is not one dimensional. Mastering finances is a multifaceted approach, requiring many needed aspects. I wanted to share with you what has worked for me because I know people can benefit from it if they choose to. If you are broke and your system isn't working then consider a change. If you are hacking away at debt and making smart financial decisions, keep up the good work. I believe this book is for everyone, although not everyone will agree with it.

I didn't write it to please every reader, but to help every reader. If you want to live like a financial rock star, then do it! God gave us free will, and you certainly don't need my financial blessing. But if you need a boost on how to get started towards freedom then I recommend doing these next steps in order. If you want it, make the decision to go for it, then fight for it with a ferocity that determines not to fail.

1. Your first step towards freedom is changing your financial mindset. Freedom is good, debt is bad. Don't compromise this mindset —there will always be negative influences in our culture at large or by your broke, broke friend. Be a leader. There is a reason your broke friend is broke.

2. Sit down and make a budget. If you are married, come up with a budget together. Communicate and focus on teamwork. Establishing a budget is mandatory if you want to improve your spending habits. You will be shocked at how much you spend, and how quickly wants can come to be perceived as needs. I encourage married couples to get a blank piece of paper. Write wants on one side of the paper and needs on the other. Then dissect your expenses and place them under the proper category. Pick one want you routinely spend money on that you can do without. Make it a competition to see who can spend the least amount on that want. Use common sense, don't spend more than you make.

3. If you are driving a car you can't afford and borrowing money to do so, downsize. Sell or trade it in then buy a modest used car with cash. Driving a modest vehicle paid for with cash was the single biggest reason we were able to pay off our house loan and become debt free at the age of 37.

4. After successfully cutting a want out of your life and budget, place that money you were spending on these things into a savings account by means of direct deposit. For example, if you cut the $75 cable/satellite TV bill out of your life, reroute that $75 directly into your savings account. Save enough cash that would allow you and your family to survive at least three months without income. You don't have to wait until your savings account is fully funded with three months of income to start the next battle.

5. This battle is to have a rainy-day fund in the amount it would cost to replace your vehicle transmission or your furnace, whichever is higher. If you have a second vehicle you only drive on Sunday, or

a motorcycle or snowmobile you could sell to get enough to launch your rainy day fund, then do it. If you don't have anything to sell, which I doubt, then start saving. This is one step in a big plan to win with money. I don't want you to be halfway to your financial goal and have the transmission go out. We don't need to go backwards by borrowing to fix something we *know* will *eventually break*. Your toys can go if you are serious about freedom. Let me be clear, this cash is for any emergency and not just your furnace or transmission. This gives you a starting point. If you are not sure how much a transmission or furnace costs, then please do some research to find out. It might open your eyes at how much money you need to have in that fund. Place this cash where you will not be tempted to use it. You will have many rainy days in your life, don't make it a flood.

6. Hopefully you can get through steps 1 through 5 quickly because they are very important. Abraham Lincoln said, "If I had 8 hours to chop down a tree, I'd spend 6 sharpening my axe." We sharpened our axe, now it's time to start chopping. Get rid of your debt, excluding your mortgage. Credit card debt and student loans have to go. Have a written plan to attack your debt and execute those plans. You are different now. You will not accept the old you or being average. By this point you are focused and can't be stopped. Keep up the good work.

7. Make sure to invest at least ten percent of your take home pay. From this point on I suggest placing every raise or bonus towards your investments, hopefully going beyond the 10 percent minimum. Let compound interest do the work, you have worked hard enough. For beginners, I strongly suggest an S&P 500 index fund / exchange traded fund or a solid performing mutual fund. You can decide what

direction you want to go later, but don't let another day go to waste trying to decide what to invest in. It is hard to outperform the market and time is on your side.

8. After erasing all debt besides your mortgage, and you've begun investing, start paying extra on your mortgage principal. If you don't own a house, be sure not to overspend on a future home. When buying a new house keep this advice in mind. If you can't afford the monthly payments of a 15-year fixed rate mortgage, you can't afford the house. Be disciplined and don't compromise on that. A good rule of thumb is to never allow your mortgage to be more than 30% of your take home pay. Remember, we don't need as much as we think we need, we just want it. If it helps, envision my luxurious 8 by 8 plywood suite I lived in for seven months while stationed in Iraq.

9. During steps 1-8, it is important to remember why you are committed to being good with money. Don't let these personal financial goals cloud your judgement to where it causes you to become focused only on yourself. Be a good steward of money and think of others. Tithe and put your trust in God. Remember, if one prospers, we all prosper.

Throughout this process be sure to take time often to remember why you are trying to achieve financial freedom and wealth. If your goal is to have financial freedom with your family, keep a picture of your family with you at all times. Look at it often. Make a silent promise to them about making good financial decisions. If you follow these steps you will gain wealth, hopefully for the right reasons.

1 Timothy 6:17-18, *"Teach those who are rich in this world not to be proud and not to trust in their money, which is so unreliable. Their trust should be in God, who richly gives us all we need for our enjoyment. Tell them to use their money to do good."*

ACKNOWLEDGEMENTS

To my amazing parents who perfectly balanced the right amount of discipline and freedom. I don't know how you did it, but I hope God hears my prayers to be like you. I truly can't thank you enough. You both taught me what love is, and that is exactly what you need from parents. I hope I can pass that on. Mom, thank you for showing me what strength and courage are. I'm closer with God due to your unbreakable faith in your last days. Dad, thanks for always being there for me, sharing your wisdom, demonstrating faith, courage, patience, and being the glue of our family. Thank you for your recommendations while reviewing my book. I love you both.

Meeting my beautiful wife was the best thing to happen to me. For some unknown reason, her love for me is unconditional. She reminds me how strong love can truly be, and how it should be. I'm forever thankful I met you and I look forward to spending the rest of my life with you. I'm grateful that God made you.

Thank you to my wonderful boys. You won't understand how much we love you until you have children of your own. You are miracles and blessings, which I knew from the moment I heard your heart beat. I'm forever thankful to God for you guys. I pray for you continually, and words truly can't explain how much I love you all.

Thank you to Pastor Mark and his wonderful wife Cindy. You guys have been amazing to me, and are truly amazing people. Thank you for allowing me to marry your daughter and raising her perfectly.

Mark, you not only taught me numerous life lessons, you also added tons of value to this book. Thank you.

Thank you Adam for all the advice you have given me throughout the years. You are always willing to help me, which is very honorable. Thank you for reading my book, making grammar corrections, and giving advice. You have always been a great brother and I love you.

To Jenna Podjasek MD, my sister and author of *Particles In The Air*. Thank you very much for your coaching, writing advice, grammar corrections, and author support. Thank you so much for the countless hours you have volunteered. You are a great sister, I love you.

Thank you Angie, Noah, Josh, Brennan, and Claire for being awesome family members. I love you all.

Thank you for all the dedicated leaders within the Marine Corps from the recruiters office, Drill Instructors, and all the Marines I have served with in M.A.P. Asylum, along with the rest of the warriors within the Mad Ghosts. Semper Fidelis.

Thank you to my brothers and sisters in Blue. Blessed are the peacemakers. By watching you all, I have learned the real meaning of the words selfless protector.

I thank God for bringing all these wonderful people in my life. I'm truly blessed and I hope I show you enough gratitude.

Thank you to Chaplain Danny Lynchard, Pastor Gunnar Hanson, Pastor Tom Zobrist, and Bill McDonald Jr. for supporting and believing in my mission. Thank you Jack Minor for your editing and additions to the book. Semper Fidelis.

ABOUT THE AUTHOR

Nate James was raised in a small town in northern Illinois. He is a graduate of Arizona State University, a retired radio operator in the United States Marine Corps, Police Officer, and most importantly, a family man.

James is happily married to his noble wife, and together they have 3 wonderful children. The James' are completely debt-free and are enjoying the benefits of financial freedom.

I hope you enjoyed fighting for your financial freedom with me.

Please consider leaving a review at: Amazon.com *-Fight For It Financial-* and visit https://www.amazon.com/author/natejames385